PROPHETS OF SALVATION

PROPHETS
OF SALVATION

Eugene H. Maly

HERDER AND HERDER

1967
HERDER AND HERDER NEW YORK
232 Madison Avenue, New York 10016

Nihil obstat: Ralph A. Aspian
Imprimatur: Edward A. McCarthy, Vicar General
Archdiocese of Cincinnati, October 5, 1966

TO THE FACULTY AND STUDENTS
of Mt. St. Mary's of the West

CONTENTS

Preface   9

1. OF PROPHETS AND PROPHECY   13
   The Beginning of the Prophetic Movement in Israel   20
   The Prophets and History   23

2. PROPHET AND WORD   30

3. THREE NON-WRITING PROPHETS   47
   Nathan and David   47
   Elijah, Champion of Truth   51
   Elisha, God's Wonder-Worker   56

4. AMOS, HOSEA, MICAH   62
   Amos, Shepherd and Prophet   62
   Hosea, Prophet of Divine Love   68
   Micah of Moresheth, Prophet of the Poor   75

5. ISAIAH   82
   Isaiah's Call to Prophecy   82
   Isaiah and Religion in Judah   86
   Isaiah and the Messianic Prince   93
   Isaiah and the Nations   99

7

CONTENTS

6. JEREMIAH ... 105
   Jeremiah's Inaugural Vision ... 105
   Jeremiah Against the Nations ... 111
   Jeremiah and the New Covenant ... 116
   Jeremiah's Contribution to Revelation ... 120

7. ZEPHANIAH, NAHUM, HABAKKUK ... 126
   Zephaniah and the Day of the Lord ... 126
   Nahum, Habakkuk and the Judgment of God ... 131

8. EZEKIEL ... 138
   The Call of Ezekiel ... 138
   Ezekiel and the Doom to Come ... 143
   Ezekiel and Salvation ... 149

9. SECOND ISAIAH ... 155
   Prophet in Exile ... 155
   The Suffering Servant ... 161

10. POST-EXILIC PROPHETS ... 168
    Haggai and Zechariah, Prophets of the New Beginning ... 168
    Obadiah, Denouncer of Edom ... 176
    Joel, Prophet of the Spirit ... 179
    Malachi and the Perfect Sacrifice ... 185

PREFACE

The great contribution made by the modern biblical revival is an appreciation of the historical character of biblical revelation. History is not some kind of disposable envelope in which revelation was given, but is of its very essence. By reason of the divine intervention in, and consequent divine "adoption" of, time and history, these now have an intrinsic value that is never lost. This means, too, that the overriding divine plan confers an organic unity on all history that links the history of the prophets in a real way with that of Jesus Christ and of His Church. In other words, the prophets are meaningful today precisely to the extent in which they were involved in the events of their own day.

It is this contemporary involvement that we wish to stress here. Too often in the past the prophets were studied in an historical vacuum. Their Christian relevance was sought without sufficient concern for their proper, contemporary relevance. As a result, much of the prophetic writing was ignored as meaningless and the remainder was given a false context that rendered it just as meaningless. Happily, the scholars have restored the prophets to their proper place in the evolving history of the divine plan of salvation. Here they are seen as living, dynamic forces in a social, cultural, political and religious context that is true to life. The prophets were men involved in their times, and it is as such that they can speak to us. It is hoped that the following pages will be a helpful vehicle for their words.

The Hebrew form of spelling proper names, as followed for example in the *Revised Standard Version,* has been used here. This is the generally recognized form today and will eventually be almost universally adopted. Since the *Confraternity of Christian Doctrine* text, which we have followed, has not yet adopted this spelling, there will be an occasional inconsistency when a proper name or noun occurs in a directly quoted passage. We trust that this will not prove too much a distraction to the reader.

A couple of the traditional names among the prophets will not be found here. It is generally recognized today that the book of *Daniel* belongs to the category of apocalyptic literature, not to that of prophecy. And *Jonah* is more properly designated didactic fiction than prophecy. For these reasons the two were not given individual attention; the concern was with the prophets strictly so called.

The short studies of the individual prophets offered here originally appeared in *Hi-Time* magazine. Miss Henriette Mackin, the publisher, has been kind enough to permit their republication in the present form; I am deeply grateful to her. The studies have been rather thoroughly revised in order to appeal to a wider audience.

No one is, or should be, more aware of the limitations of a book than its author. Certainly in the present case no claims are made to any contribution to scholarly work on the prophets. The sole purpose of the book is to make the prophets of ancient Israel live again through their own words, to present them in a way that will make them meaningful to a twentieth-century civilization.

PROPHETS OF SALVATION

1.

OF PROPHETS AND PROPHECY

Deep in the heart of every man there are implanted certain basic convictions, ideals, instincts. Despite the varying external forms in which they are expressed, they are recognizable in the consistency of their assertion. The very existence of a world of the divine is a clear example of this. In response to an inner insistence of his being, man has, with formidable regularity, asserted the existence of a God. He may see Him expressed in the glowing sun or the mighty river or the invisible Lord of history, —but he is convinced there is a God. From this conviction religion is born.

Religion concerns the relationship between man and God, regulating the forms of its expression. And here, too, we find a remarkable community of convictions. The races of man have consistently agreed that our world is influenced in some way or another by God, that this God is to be worshipped, that sacrifice is an eminent form of this worship. It is, moreover, the common belief of mankind that certain individuals are called to be the intermediaries, the moderators, or, in varying forms, the ministers of the divine-human relationship. If they offer sacrifice and ask God's blessings on the people, they are called priests. If they are the vehicles of God's message, of His infallible and all-powerful word, they are called prophets.

Prophetism is common to many religions. And yet the biblical prophet is a unique phenomenon in the history of religion. In the resolution of this apparent contradiction we will gain an understanding and appreciation of the prophetic movement in Israel.

What is a prophet in the biblical sense? The question is not an idle one. Two factors in particular have conditioned our understanding of the word, an understanding which is not at all biblical. The first factor is the popular use of the word in the sense of one who predicts future events. It is not difficult to see how such a definition should have gained currency. Granted the basic concept that a prophet has something to do with divine revelation and granted the human propensity to curiosity about the future, the idea was easily encouraged that the prophet will satisfy that curiosity. It was, perhaps, a more refined conviction than that which opted for sheep's livers, tea leaves or crystal balls, but it reflects basically the same mentality.

The other factor influencing the currency of this definition was a religious one and endemic to a particular approach of Catholic apologetics of the past era. This was a wholly defensive approach wherein every attempt was made to prove as conclusively as possible the legitimacy of the Christian, and specifically the Catholic claim. After the evidence of historical charts and irrefutable miracles had made its inroads on the unbeliever's position, the Old Testament prophets were called upon to deliver the final blow in the form of detailed predictions of what would happen from eight to five hundred years after their day. Because of the rather bad repute that biblical studies had otherwise enjoyed during this same period, a repute fostered by the false philosophical postulates of the chief practitioners of the biblical sciences, any other use of the Bible was fairly effectively, if not officially, discouraged. Hence the prophetic contribution to religion remained restricted to the predictive element and this was grossly exaggerated beyond its proper dimensions.

Thus the situation remained and thus a mentality developed among Catholic people and Catholic priests. Only the freeing of the Bible from its contamination with rationalism and the consequent freeing of the biblical scholar led to a more accurate appraisal of the prophet's role, and, even better, of the prophetic movement.

Both etymologically and historically, it was discovered, the prophet was not one who predicted future events, but one who was called by God to speak for God. A prophet, then, is a divine spokesman and, as such, he frequently has more urgent business to attend to than providing jigsaw pieces for a picture of future history. And even when he does provide such pieces, they are always so intimately connected with the contemporary scene that it is not possible at times to recognize their value as jigsaw pieces. The maid of *Isaiah* 7:14 will in truth be a valuable addition to Matthew's messianic picture, but the maid of *Isaiah* 7:14 was also a very live issue of Isaiah's own day.

With these necessary clarifications made, we can see now why the biblical concept of prophet, as a spokesman of God, could be shared by many other peoples. All peoples of the ancient Near East were religious; all had a "revelation," whether based on the phenomena of nature, as in the case of the pagan peoples, or on the historical events, as in the case of the Hebrews. All, therefore, had religious men whose mission it was to interpret the divine will. All had prophets; India's *fakir,* classical China's sage, Arabia's *kahin,* ancient Egypt's lector-priest, and Israel's *nabi* all had this in common, that they claimed to be the bearers of the divine message.

Obviously, not all prophets are prophets of the one true God, nor do all bear the same message, nor do all deliver their message in similar forms. We shall see shortly that, while there are distinguishable parallels among the prophets of mankind, there are also marked differences which, in Israel's case, constitute her prophets as unique. But at least we can say that common to every man is the need for prophets and for prophecy, the inextinguishable yearning of the human heart to hear God's word spoken with authority. That even pagans should have their prophets is telling evidence.

But besides sharing a common function, these old world prophets also shared, in many ways, a common method. In *1 Kings* 18 we read about the prophets of Baal, the god of Jezebel, pagan queen brought from Tyre by her husband Ahab. The actions these prophets performed seem exceedingly strange to us. They danced about, apparently to such an extent that they went into a frenzy. Again, we read in an ancient tale of adventure about an ambassador from Egypt who related a story of a young man in a royal court where he was staying. The young man, we are told, was seized by the god and spoke as though he were inspired.

A glance at the prophetic phenomenon in Israel will reveal something not too dissimilar, at least in the beginning of the movement. We read in *1 Samuel* 10:5 of "a band of prophets coming down from the high place with harp, tambourine, flute, and lyre before them, prophesying." This last word is a probable reference to a sort of ecstatic chattering, analogous, perhaps, to the glossalalia of the early Christian community. We read further that, when Saul met this band of prophets and experienced their prophesying, ". . . the spirit of God came mightily upon him . . ." (1 Sam 10:10) in accord with the promise of Samuel that he would "prophesy with them and be turned into another man" (1 Sam 10:6) Saul, in other words, was in a state of frenzy that would not be entirely unlike the condition of the pagan prophets of Baal.

We will be shocked or not at this similarity of prophetic expression, depending on the keenness of our historical sense. History has sufficient records of God's adaptation of His revelation to the customs and mentality of the contemporary world to prepare the serious student for this particular adaptation. These men of ancient Israel felt the action of God upon them. They felt also the need to surrender themselves completely to that divine action. The external actions of singing, dancing and "prophesying" are the expression of that need. They were actions in conformity with the culture of the age and used by God for His purposes. The prophetic action, we know, became more sophisticated in a later period, but always in conformity with the development of Israelite religion and culture. We must add, in fairness to the primitive prophets of Israel, that there is no evidence that they adopted the cruder manifestations among their separated brethren of the Canaanite faith. The prophets of Baal, we learn, "cut themselves after their custom with swords and lances, until the blood gushed out upon them" (1 Kgs 18:28). The sacred author's delicate phrasing, "after their custom," is sign enough that he found no such barbarisms in Israel.

We might pause here for a moment to ask ourselves the meaning behind these actions. Among the pagans it was to dispose the god to reveal himself. Some scholars think that the purpose of the cutting with knives was to excite the pity of the god on the one who was bleeding and so to make himself known. Moreover, since the gods were such mysterious beings for the

17

pagans, they thought it quite proper for man to be in a state of ecstatic frenzy, to be out of his senses, before he could receive and understand their revelations.

To seek out the divine intention or to occasion the manifestation of properly divine power by occult means was a preoccupation common to the ancient Near East. The concern is, we readily admit, understandable enough. What is difficult for us of the twentieth century to understand is the method used to attain that end. We see, for example, no adequate connection between the state of a sheep's liver and the fate of an individual, and we rightly call the practice based on a presumed connection superstition. It is, of course, just as superstitious to think that God has revealed His will in a handful of tea leaves or in the position of the stars. And yet tea leaves and horoscopes have been endowed with a certain glamour in the context of the modern breakfast table. Superstitions die hard.

But behind the superstition there does lie a conviction that we cannot simply ignore. It is a conviction that there is a God who is responsible for what happens on earth and that the knowledge of the divine will is a matter of extreme importance. There are several things that man can do about this conviction. He can devise human means for ascertaining the divine will, such as cutting himself, reading sheep's livers, tea leaves or horoscopes. Unfortunately, these *are* human means and will do little good. The prophets of Baal tried the first method and failed miserably; others throughout history have tried the other methods and have done no better.

Realizing, therefore, that human means will never be able to explore the world of God, man might be tempted to despair of ever learning about God's will. He might say that he must get

18

along the best he can without knowing what God's will really is. This, at least, is better than being deceived by the superstitions of the astrologists or the examiners of odd bits of nature.

There is, however, one more attitude possible in the face of the common conviction. That is to grant, first of all, God's ability to reveal His will to man. Then, on the reasonable supposition that God has an interest in man, we can establish the reasonable hypothesis that He *has* revealed His will. It is for the reasonable man, then, to examine the history of religions and ask whether such a revelation has taken place in the past. His task might seem enormous. But he can reject immediately those "revelations" which he clearly sees as the result of superstitious practices. Similarly will he be suspicious of those prophets who are always saying what man wants to hear; man needs no prophet to acquire that information.

And so, after hearing the case of the prophets of Baal and of the other pagan gods, the reasonable man will hear the case of the prophets of Israel. Even a preliminary glimpse indicates that their case will be more than worth the hearing. After all, the prophets of Israel preached a message that has been listened to for some three thousand years. In the league of the prophets that is an enviable and completely unparalleled record. In fact, were it not for the archaeologist's spade, it is unlikely that we would ever know how extensive the international league of ancient prophets was. Except within Israel the prophetic messages had died and been buried along with the prophets who spoke them. The prophets of Israel and their message were altogether different.

This brings us, then, to the second part of our paradox. What was it that constituted the biblical prophet a unique phenomenon in the history of religion? Briefly, the difference lies wholly in the divinity for whom he was a spokesman. His God was a unique God, and this made him necessarily a unique prophet. Because his God was the Lord of all men whose will was steadfast, the biblical prophet could speak with an authority that defied priest and monarch alike. Because his God was the supreme master of history's unfolding, the biblical prophet could interpret that unfolding infallibly. This conclusion, we must be sure, rests on the analysis of the prophets themselves and of their oracles; we do not learn of it in some inspired introduction to the prophetic movement. It is only by reading the prophets and appreciating the extraordinary character of their faith that we are led inevitably to the God who spoke through them.

THE BEGINNING OF THE PROPHETIC
MOVEMENT IN ISRAEL

The best means of appreciating the uniqueness of Israel's prophets, therefore, is by meeting them and getting to know them. Obviously, we can do little more than effect an introduction in these pages. And we must begin with the first appearance of the prophetic phenomenon on Israel's historical scene. The role of the prophet there will teach us the role of the man of God in every period of religious crisis.

The first appearance of the prophets in Israel as a group has already been alluded to. It was the group with whom Saul, the first king of Israel, had come into contact and with whom he identified himself by his actions. The appearance indicates a movement, a tendency to promote something or to denounce something. When serious men get together and perform extraordinary actions, there must be a reason for it. Since it is a religious movement, we might suspect that some religious malaise lay at the root of it. We do not have to look very far to find it.

The Ark of the Covenant, the symbol of Israel's religious unity under Yahweh, was kept at the time of Samuel at Shiloh. (We are in the latter part of the eleventh century, towards the close of the period of the judges.) Eli was the priest in charge of this most important shrine and amphictyonic center. (The amphictyony was the league of twelve tribes, known as Israel and banded together in common allegiance to Yahweh.) As was the custom in those days, his sons, too, acted as priests and assisted their father at the shrine.

Somehow, as happens periodically in mankind's religious history, a spirit of irresponsibility and moral degeneration had entered into Eli's sons. They acted contemptuously with the people, committed open sins of impurity and, in general, debased the priestly office. A very black picture of the priesthood of that day is painted in the second chapter of *1 Samuel*. The very length of the description of their crimes shows how seriously the evil was looked upon by those who fashioned the original account and by its final editors.

Nor was this spirit of social irresponsibility and moral perversion confined to the priesthood. We read that even Samuel's sons did not walk in his ways. He had appointed them judges like himself, but they "turned aside after gain; they took bribes and perverted justice" (1 Sam 8:1–3). But the faults of public officials, like the faults of the clergy, are quickly bruited about. When the people, therefore, came to Samuel and demanded a king, they told him bluntly, "Behold, you are old and your sons do not walk in your ways" (1 Sam 8:5).

21

It was at this critical period in Israel's religious history, a period sadly in need of reform, that we first meet the prophets. That they were raised up by God to meet the challenge of the day there is no reason for doubting. Dr. William F. Albright has compared their appearance at this crucial moment to the rise of the mendicant orders in medieval Catholicism. Both were responses to the challenge of a corrupt clergy and of declining religious ideals. Both provided the needed ferment to awaken ancient ideals. Just how these early prophets went about the work of reform we cannot, unfortunately, say in detail; the biblical records are rather spare on this point. We might conjecture, however, that the actions they performed were intended to draw the people to them, to make them aware of the spirit of God working in them, and to encourage them to imitate their lives of dedication to the one true God. No doubt they uttered words of praise of God and words of warning, too, all of it designed to keep alive the spirit of reform.

In God's providence the movement did not die out. It was to continue and produce some of the greatest men of the Old Testament. The prophets of a later age would differ in many respects from those ecstatic prophets of Samuel's age. But the same divine vocation and the same divine mission of reform were always present. These were sufficient to establish a continuity between the two groups. It was a bond that was stronger than any external bond of similarity of action. We might compare it with the bond that unites us with the earliest Christians. Even though we may not express our convictions by "speaking in tongues" as did the early Christians, the bond of unity in the Mystical Body is just as surely there.

One more observation needs making here. The prophetic

movement arose in Israel around the same time as did the monarchy. Saul, the first king, meets a group of the first prophets and comes under their influence. Prophecy and kingship confront one another in their beginnings. They would continue to confront one another throughout their respective histories. Indeed, much of the history of prophecy is determined by the history of kingship.

THE PROPHETS AND HISTORY

This introduces another characteristic of the Israelite prophet, the relevance of prophecy to history and to historical time. Like any heir of Israel's faith, the prophet was convinced of the unity of history, a unity measured by the overriding plan of the intervening God. For this reason the prophet was, as we have seen, a man whose vision was open to the future, because that future was God's. And so sure were they that it was God's future that, in describing it, they could use a past tense of the verb. For the prophet the future shared the absolute certainty of the past.

But the prophet's message was much more surely tied to the past, to that past when God saved His people, bringing them up out of Egypt and binding them to Him in the solemn covenant of Sinai. This was the golden age of the people's life with God. The past was the norm of God's action in the future, the norm, too, of Israel's response in covenant love.

The prophets were above all, however, men of the present. In one word, the prophets were involved. They were men of their times. It is this involvement in the present life of their people that made them the great men that they were. If they looked to the past, it was not like some attic recluse who refuses to face life. It was, as we have seen, because the past was the best criterion for making a judgment on Israel's present. And if they looked to the future, again it was not to live in a dream world of their own making. It was to paint a picture of all that would inevitably flow from the present conduct of the people and to arouse in their hardened hearts a present sense of hope and turn them to their God again. The realism of the prophets was of the hardheaded variety that knew that God's interest in the world had changed all values and all standards.

It is in the context of the biblical view of history, a view determined by the conviction of a supreme moral Lord intervening in history and giving it meaning and direction, that some of the most profound insights of the prophets were generated. Convinced that Israel had been elected and called to greatness—a conviction born in the assurance that it was on no merits of their own that Yahweh had saved them—the prophets gradually developed an eschatology, and within its framework a messianism that would be extremely important for the development of Old Testament revelation.

It is understandable that the earliest expressions of an eschatology—in the very broad sense of a climax being reached in this divinely directed history, but without the necessity of another special divine intervention as in the past—should be centered around the Davidic kingdom. We are familiar with the prophetic statement in *Genesis* 49:8–12 which depicts the hegemony of the tribe of Judah over the other tribes. This was likely composed during the reign of David or of Solomon and is a witness to a future hope that is based on the present brilliant reign of David. Similar in form is the oracle in *Numbers* 24:15–19, possibly composed at an even earlier date than that of *Genesis* and expressing again, but in less specific terms, the conviction of future national greatness.

When we come to the classical prophets of the eighth, seventh and sixth centuries, there are already some vast developments that have taken place. For one thing the eschatological hope has introduced the concept of the "day of Yahweh," or the "day of the Lord." In other words, the climax of history would witness some manifestation of God, a manifestation similar to that of His intervention at the time of the exodus. However, we must beware of oversimplifying the concept to the extent that, wherever we find the expression "day of the Lord," we see the conviction of a cataclysmic intervention that will usher in a new period, a new history that will never end. In the earlier period we can be fairly sure that the expression referred only to the climactic development of the present history.

Another development that had taken place and that is most important for understanding the prophetic message is the moral corruption of the people. This was attended by, both as cause and effect, a syncretistic expression of their faith, in which pagan elements were introduced into their worship of Yahweh, or by open idolatry. The covenant, which had bound them by ties of love and loyalty to Yahweh, far from acting as a restraining influence on some of them, actually became the occasion for much of the moral perversion. They had developed the notion that Yahweh's steadfast love and faithfulness to His promises guaranteed their protection from harm and their assurance of national glory. The moral stipulations that were the necessary part of their response to the covenant were forgotten, and in their place there was substituted a ritual worship which was vitiated by formalism. Unless we have a full understanding of this situation in the times of the prophets we cannot appreciate their message. And to the extent that the same situation exists in the various periods of Christian history, to that same extent is the prophetic message still relevant.

By the time of the prophet Amos, the shepherd of Tekoa called from his native Judah to bring God's word to the northern kingdom in the eighth century, the expression "day of the Lord" was already current. And from the words of Amos we know in what sense it was understood. "Woe to you," he says, "who desire the day of the Lord! Why would you have the day of the Lord? It is darkness, and not light" (Am 5:18). It is clear that the people of the North looked forward to that day as the justification of Israel and the climax of their salvation. Amos saw it in completely opposite terms. It was a day of darkness, a day in which Yahweh would expend His wrath on His people precisely because of their special election. Amos was not a complete pessimist. In his very plea for conversion (5:4–6. 14–15) there is implicit a future salvation, even though the explicit description found at the end of the book is a later addition.

It is obvious, however, that if Amos's thought of a day of the Lord were developed even further there would gradually come about the conviction of the need for a new intervention of Yahweh that would effect salvation, an eschatology in the strictest sense. Just when it was developed is most difficult to say. But reading the prophets, looking for the expressions of an eschatology and trying to determine their precise meaning will contribute to a more fruitful understanding of them. In *Isaiah* 2:6–22 we find the notion of Amos developed to the extent that the day of the Lord is seen as a day when He will stretch forth His arm in anger not only against His own rebellious people, but also "against all that is proud and lofty, against all that is lifted up and high." And in the post-exilic prophet Joel we find the day of the Lord described in eschatological terminology of the strictest proportion. It is the *dies irae, dies illa* from which the Sequence for the Requiem Mass borrowed much of its imagery.

It is within this broad framework of the coming day of the Lord that the messianic note was similarly developed. And there are parallels in the development. The hope in the beginning centered around the Davidic dynasty; it was a hope for national glory. Dominant in the prophecies of *Isaiah,* it is still formulated in those of *Jeremiah* and *Ezekiel,* although in the latter two we do find an increasing emphasis on the spiritual elements of the messianic future. With the exile there came a complete dashing of all the hopes of the past, a catastrophe whose significance for the chosen people it is almost impossible for us to conceive. For many it led to a complete abandonment of their ancient faith. For the remnant it meant a complete revamping of the expression of their hope. One of the most profound of these was the picture of the suffering servant of Yahweh, painted by an anonymous prophet of the exile who thereby introduced the notion of vicarious suffering into the theology of the Old Testament, and left a rich heritage that the New Testament writers were to exploit to the fullest extent in their attempts to explain the mystery of Jesus Christ. We will meet this extraordinary figure in a future chapter. Again, after the exile the royal messianic hope flared again for a while, as evidenced in the prophet Zechariah and possibly in some of the additions to the pre-exilic prophets. But when the eschatological development of the post-exilic period reached its height in the apocalyptic period of the last two centuries before Christ, we find the messianic note expressed in the form of a transcendental "Son of man" in *Daniel* 7:13–14.

We have not tried to present the prophetic development of messianism, as is obvious. All we have wanted to do is to provide some kind of guidelines for the study of the individual prophets that follows. As we have insisted, the understanding of this messianism in the prophets is intimately linked with the contemporary situation and must not be divorced from it. The prophetic picture of the future is both determined by the shaping of the history of their own world, a shaping for which they see the people as responsible inasmuch as they obey or refuse to obey the word of the Lord spoken first on Sinai and now repeated through the prophets' mouth, and colored by the imagery of their own world. As we have seen, the coloring will change as the world of the prophets changes. It is not the essential element of their message.

The Old Testament is nothing more than the story of God's covenant with Israel. The covenant, then, has a central place in the biblical revelation of the Old Testament. If so, we would expect that the covenant would mean much to the prophets too. Again, we cannot go into any detail here concerning the development of the covenant idea in the individual prophets. It is one of those concepts that the reader should have constantly in the background as he studies the prophets and tries to catch the varied expression of it in the prophetic message. Not all of the prophets, of course, gave it the same value. For Hosea, the prophet of the north, it was the instrument of God's love for His people that surpassed all understanding. And because of his conviction of that love, he expressed the covenant love of God for Israel in figures that became classic in biblical literature. Jeremiah, too, understood the meaning of the covenant love, and for him it found expression in the conviction of a new covenant that God would make with His people in which the stipulations, the *reactio humana* to the *actio divina* which Israel had failed to make, would be written in the hearts of men so that it would no longer be necessary for a man to teach his neighbor to know the Lord, "for they shall all know me, from the least of them to the greatest, says the Lord" (Jer 31:31–34).

The prophetic movement continued on into the post-exilic period, but it had lost much of its force by that time. It still played an important role in giving courage to the community returned from exile, but for the most part its task had been accomplished. Ethical monotheism, with all that it implied in the way of social justice, morality and purity of worship, had been securely established among the remnant. Its task would now be taken over, in large part, by the Torah. Then would come the fullness of times when the first stage in the realization of the eschatological future would be fulfilled. Until then it can be said that no group of men in the history of mankind had stood forth so fearlessly and, in the end, so effectively, for the rights of God and of man.

2.

PROPHET AND WORD

WE have spoken of the prophet and of the prophetic movement in Israel. But before considering the individual prophets something deserves to be said about the word spoken by the prophet and how it is to be determined as God's word. We have seen that the principal difference between Israel's prophets and those of other peoples was in the God they represented. This difference would inevitably affect the word they spoke.

The word is one of the most neglected concepts in modern western civilization. Doubtless, the abuse of the word in both its oral and its printed forms accounts for much of this. More radically it can be traced to the Greek philosophical influence on our civilization. The "essentialism" of the philosophers has encouraged that kind of analysis that results in dichotomies—the dichotomy, for example, in man between body and soul, in most created beings between matter and form and, in our area, between the idea and the word that clothes it. We recommend no wholesale abandonment of essentialism here; we wish merely to point out its deficiencies. One of these is that the world of ideas has been extolled to the almost total ignoring and consequent impoverishment of the world of words.

The word has been conceived as a kind of transient vehicle of the idea, so transient, in fact, that its worth has been depreciated beyond all reason. Perhaps because of this we manufacture words effortlessly and in abundance and the lack of effort is evident in the very abundance. The idea reigns supreme; the word is spurned as inconsequential.

Yet even the logical analysis of the philosopher should teach us that this analysis is not worthy of the word. The word is more than a transient vehicle; the word *is* the idea in act. Without the word the idea remains hidden and valueless to the world outside. It is the word that empowers it, enabling it to have its influence on a whole world of men. And the force of the word is awesome. Spoken in anger it can rouse passions that can lead to injury, even death. Spoken with zeal and enthusiasm it can change hearts and lives or it can start revolutions. Spoken in love the word can transform a world.

The biblical writers saw clearly this power of the human word. While they may not have analyzed it as we can, they expressed it clearly in their writings. Recall the incident in *Genesis* where Jacob, through deception, receives from his father Isaac the blessing of the first-born. Afterwards Esau enters, unaware of what has transpired, and asks for the same blessing. Isaac comes to understand what has taken place and cries out that he is unable to bless Esau as the first-born. That word of blessing had already been drawn from the innermost reaches of his being, had gone forth from his mouth and had entered into the being of Jacob. There is nothing, then, that Isaac can do: "I have appointed him your lord, and have given him all his brothers as servants. I have enriched him with grain and wine . . ." (Gn 27:37). The patriarch speaks as though the inheritance had already been transferred to Jacob. In a sense it had, in the word that was spoken. Esau himself recognized the finality of the blessing and he "wept aloud."

31

This biblical concept of the word is further illustrated in the Hebrew term for "word." *Dabar* means not only "word" but also "thing," and so gives striking confirmation to the concrete manner in which they envisioned the word as a material reality created within the human agent and going forth into the world to have its effect. It follows from this that the greater the person who creates the word, the greater is the word itself. The word of the patriarch, it goes without saying, was considered among the most powerful of human words.

It is in the light of this consideration of the human word that we can begin to appreciate the biblical concept of the divine word. The most dramatic illustration of the power of God's word is surely found in the priestly story of creation in *Genesis* 1. The author was faced with the formidable task of showing how the transcendent and holy Lord had bridged the enormous gap between himself and created being. Unlike the earlier Yahwist author who spoke freely of God coming down and forming man out of the dust of the ground, our priestly author could not bring himself to suggest in such a way a contamination of the "otherness" of God. He spoke, therefore, of God's word going forth to bridge the gap: "God said, 'Let there be light,' and there was light" (Gn 1:3). God spoke a word, and so powerful was that word that its effect was to produce immediately all that was implied in it. We read: "God saw that the light was good." By this the author tells us that what was created by the word was in perfect correspondence with all that God had intended by it. Such is the power of the divine word.

But God's word does more than create nature and all the objects we see about us; it also creates history. It requires a bit of thought to understand this, but it is worth the effort. It is necessary if we want to understand the prophets.

We speak freely these days of salvation history. This is not said as a complaint. But we should appreciate more deeply than we probably do the profound implications of the expression. Most profound of all is that this history is God's history, pregnant with His purpose and with His power to achieve it. It is because of this alone that it can be called *salvation* history, for its capacity to save is divine in origin and in realization. It is a history that supposes the free rejection by man of God's friendship once offered and the consequent involvement of man in sin and increasing corruption. Against the background of this rejection God devised a plan that we call "salvation history."

We cannot here detail the implementation of this plan. We are concerned solely with the manner in which the biblical authors portrayed the role of God's word in that history. When God speaks that word, man is free to answer or not. But so powerful is it that if man does answer and obey it, the word will produce great things in him.

An example. God spoke a word to Abraham. He told him to leave his country, his kinsfolk and his father's house, and to go to another land. If Abraham refused, the world would never know of him; he would be forgotten soon after his death. If he answered that word in obedience, he would, on God's promise, be blessed with many descendants who would form a nation. His name would be remembered forever (Gn 12:1-3). With the simplicity of total commitment to the divine speaker Abraham heard the word and obeyed it. "Abram went away as the Lord had commanded him" (Gn 12:4). The following chapters receive their interest from the tension surrounding the fulfillment of the word of promise. The barren Sarah, Ishmael born of a slave wife, the requested sacrifice of the only son Isaac—these are the elements that constitute the drama of God's word of promise.

But the inspired authors, despite the artistic ability with which they portray the tension, are themselves never in doubt. God's word *will* be achieved. And we know, of course, that it was. The unknown man from Mesopotamia became the father of the "sons of Israel" and through them do we today, some 3800 years later, still remember and revere the name of Abraham. The word of God, listened to and obeyed, had changed the course of history.

Nor was that the only time that God spoke in history. He spoke frequently to His people who, by their obedience or disobedience, became the instruments of the divine word's fashioning of history's course. An exilic prophet put it as starkly as it can be put: "For just as from the heavens the rain and snow come down and do not return there till they have watered the earth, making it fertile and fruitful, giving seed to him who sows and bread to him who eats, so shall my word be that goes forth from my mouth; it shall not return to me void, but shall do my will, achieving the end for which I sent it" (Is 55:10–11).

A tendency can be noticed in post-exilic Israel to attribute more and more of the events of the past to God's word. The tendency reaches its climax in the book of *Wisdom* whose second century B.C. author has personified the divine word in his midrashic description of the exodus. In the portrayal of the plagues he envisions the final one as the result of a decree that came down from the heavenly throne, a word from God that is depicted as a giant warrior. "For when peaceful stillness compassed everything and the night in its swift course was half spent, your all-powerful word from heaven's royal throne bounded, a fierce warrior, into the doomed land, bearing the sharp sword of your inexorable decree. And as he alighted he filled every place with death; he still reached to heaven, while he stood upon the earth" (18:14–16).

34

This rich theology of the divine word attains its perfect fulfillment only with the revelation of the perfect word of God, Jesus
Christ. The author of the epistle to the Hebrews makes explicit
the contrast between the two revelations, the imperfect one of
the Old Testament and the perfect one of the New: "God, who
at sundry times and in divers manners spoke in times past to the
fathers by the prophets, last of all in these days has spoken to us
by his Son, whom he appointed heir of all things, by whom also
he made the world . . ." (1:1–2). Jesus, then, is the last and
perfect word of the Father, the one who, as St. John tells us, was
in the beginning with God and who was God, the word that
became flesh and dwelt among us (1:1. 14).

It was to prepare for the coming of this, His final word, that
God sent His spokesmen, the prophets. And the significance that
God Himself gave to this mission can be grasped by the manner
in which He called the three major prophets, Isaiah, Jeremiah and
Ezekiel. We shall see this in slightly greater detail in the individual studies. For now it will suffice to note that in all three
cases the inaugural visions contain an explicit reference to a
special cleansing of the prophet that he might fittingly preach the
divine and awesome word. Isaiah's lips are cleansed with a burning ember taken from the altar by one of the seraphim (6:6–7).
The Lord Himself touches tenderly the lips of Jeremiah in vision
and so teaches him that he has been made capable of speaking
the Lord's word (1:9). And in the case of Ezekiel's vision a large
scroll is given him to eat. It contained the words of God to be
spoken to the people, and the prophet found the scroll sweet as
honey in his mouth (3:1–4).

With such preparation we can readily appreciate why the
prophets should have been deeply religious men zealous for
God's truth. What might seem strange is that there were those

35

prophets who were not. And yet we come across them in the Old Testament with what the pious reader might consider bewildering profusion. But the presence of false prophets, and even their relative profusion, is only one more sign of the divine concern for human freedom. God leaves man free to pervert His own word if he so chooses in order that man's response to that word might be all the more committed.

What is a false prophet? Is he one who claims to speak for God but doesn't? A good case could be made for this definition. The great prophet Jeremiah has a powerful address against this kind of prophet. Speaking in God's name he refers to them as "prophets who prophesy lies in my name." "Therefore," God continues, "I am against the prophets . . . who steal my words from each other. . . . From me they have no mission or command, and they do this people no good at all, says the Lord." The whole passage, in *Jeremiah* 23:9–32, should be read aloud to appreciate the anguish in Jeremiah's heart as he considers the evil done by these false prophets.

But it is not always possible to know whether a man is actually speaking for God or not. Is there some other way to judge him? One possibility is to study the reasons why they prophesied. Some of the great prophets, like Jeremiah and Amos, did not want to be prophets at all; they did so only because God wanted them. Amos would much rather have stayed with his flock of sheep in Tekoa, but God called him and he could not refuse (see Am 7:14–16).

Others, however, went about their work with great enthusiasm. And some of these prophesied only to win favor. They said only what their hearers wanted them to say. We read an interesting story in *3 Kings* 22 about Ahab, the king of Israel, who asked his prophets whether he should go to war against Syria. All of them told him that he should because he would be victorious. But one more prophet was brought before the king, one the king did not like because "he doth not prophesy good to me, but evil." This prophet at first told Ahab that he should go, for the Lord would make him victorious. But he was only parroting the other prophets who had spoken before him, implying that it would do no good for him to speak the truth since the king was determined to fight in any case. When the king, however, reacted in astonishment and demanded that the prophet speak truly, he then heard the words he feared he would hear, the prediction of his coming defeat. In this case it was easy to tell the true prophet from the false ones by the outcome of the battle.

In very strong language the prophet Micah writes of the "prophets who lead my people astray; who, when their teeth have something to bite, announce peace, but when one fails to put something in their mouth, proclaim war against him" (Mi 3:5). In other words, they prophesy good things to those who pay them well and evil things to others. He puts this in other words when he says a little later, ". . . her prophets divine for money" (3:11).

It probably wasn't difficult to identify false prophets of this kind. But then, people like to hear good things about themselves, so much in fact that they are even willing to pay others to say them! It is doubtful if the gazers into crystal balls or the readers of tea leaves would long remain in business if they purged their analyses of the categories of handsome young men, lost wealthy uncles and rewarding chance encounters. Similar foibles of human nature provided grist for the mills of the false prophets of the Old Testament.

Especially welcome by those who indulge in wishful thinking are the false prophets of national glory. These are the ones who, even when the outlook is bleak, tell the people that they are doing well and that the Lord is with them. They speak of even greater glory to come, and say that it is only necessary to continue as they are; the Lord will soon deliver them from the brink of defeat. Quite a few rose-colored bubbles of this kind were blown by the false prophets of ancient Israel. It took real courage to burst those bubbles, and to tell the people that the Lord was *not* with them, that things were going to get worse before they got better, that the country was even going down in defeat. It took courage, and the false prophets did not have that courage. It took men like the "timid" Jeremiah to tell the people what the false prophets cry: " 'Peace! Peace!' they say, though there is no peace" (Jer 8:11).

It is when we understand the heart of the true prophet that we are better able to recognize the false. The former was a man who, convinced that he spoke for God, made an honest judgment on the issues of his times. But that judgment was made in the light of God's covenant with Israel. It is very important, therefore, that we understand this covenant if we wish to understand the prophets of Israel.

The covenant was a pact or treaty made by God with the Hebrew people. By it they entered into a special relationship with God. They were His subjects; He was their Lord. There were certain stipulations, or commandments, that the people had to agree to if they wanted to enter into this covenant. The basic ones are contained in what we call the Ten Commandments. The Israelites were willing to accept these stipulations because of all that God had done for them. And it was implied that if they kept His commandments He would continue to protect them. "If you keep my Law I will be your God and you will be my people." This was the essence of the covenant.

Later Israel began to forget about the commandments. She did not forget about the mighty acts of God, of course, how He had saved her throughout her history. In fact, it was in looking back on that past history that the people developed the false conviction that they could never be defeated. Surely God would not abandon His own people for whom He had done so much in the past! Regardless of their response to the Lord's stipulations, He would continue to save them. The false prophets, whether consciously or unconsciously, fostered this conviction. Perhaps in some cases they were themselves deceived and thought that God was bound by His part of the covenant no matter what the people did. This is not to excuse their deception. Any man who claims so high an office as the spokesman of God must know the mind of God in those matters which concern his mission. No true prophet could ever misjudge so radically the respective roles of God and Israel in the covenant order. Such misjudgment, moreover, would almost necessarily lead to immorality in their own lives and to the encouragement of it in the lives of others. This is a frequent charge of the true prophets against their self-made imitators.

The covenant was designed by God to make His people holy. They were to keep His laws so that they might be holy as He, the Lord their God, was holy. Moreover, God was the one who had made the covenant of His own free will and who had laid down the conditions. It was an act of pure loving kindness on His part. If the people refused to abide by the conditions, God could revoke the covenant.

Perhaps, in the last analysis, this is the best way to distinguish the true prophets from the false prophets. If they were champions of the covenant, if they preached the moral law contained there no matter what the opposition was, and if they were not afraid to tell the people when they were doing wrong and violating the covenant, then they were the true prophets called by God to preach His word. But if they deceived the people by telling them that the Lord was with them no matter what they did, if they favored the wealthy and the powerful telling them what they liked to hear, and if they encouraged the violation of the covenant by their own immoral lives, then they were no true prophets of God. They were false prophets among God's people.

Anything really worth-while will always have its imitators. This is more true in religion than anywhere else, precisely because religion deals with the noblest things and makes the greatest demands on man. In the Old Testament those demands were given as words of God and were backed by the guarantee of those words. The prophet of Israel was called to preach them. But because of the character of the prophetic word, its power and its influence, there were bound to rise up in Israel false chaimants to that word.

The true prophet was aware of the high dignity of his calling. He knew what it meant to speak God's word. That is why he entered the prophetic mission with fear and trembling. That, too, explains the scorn with which they looked on their false imitators, the speakers, not of God's word, but of their own empty words. It is Jeremiah who compares the word of God to a fire, or to a hammer that shatters rocks (23:29). Speaking of the false claimants to that word he writes, "Thus says the Lord of hosts: listen not to the words of your prophets, who fill you with emptiness; visions of their own fancy they speak, not from the mouth of the Lord" (23:16).

40

The word of God spoken by the true prophet of Israel could never bear comparison with the magic word revered in other religions. The magic word makes sense only to the one who utters it; to its hearers it remains meaningless, not by reason of the hardness of their hearts but by reason of the nature of the word. Moreover, it is more wont to produce its effect only when pronounced in a special way or at a special time. In the end, there is no true relationship between the magic word and its supposed effect. Not so with God's word. There is a perfect relationship, a perfect correspondence between word and effect, for the latter is achieved not because the word is spoken here or at this special time, but simply because it is spoken, ultimately, by God. This was the conviction of the true prophets; it was the conviction of the sacred writers who have left us the record of their mission.

We shall conclude this chapter with a survey, however brief, of Israel's history. Such a survey is demanded, first of all, because that history was the context in which the prophets spoke their words. They were men deeply involved in the events of their times. We have said that they were neither attic recluses living wholly in the past nor idle dreamers of a rosy future. They were down-to-earth realists who were convinced that the world's destiny was conditioned by the divine intervention and that they had a significant part in that destiny.

In the treatment of the individual prophets we shall consider the historical background that was a necessary part of their oracles. Here we are only concerned with what we have called a survey, a general view of the entire history. Without this there is the danger that the details of history will be floating around in the readers' memories and imaginations without a solid anchor. How many Bible readers have a vivid recollection of David's prowess with the slingshot or of Solomon's tête-à-tête with the queen of Sheba, but are incapable of relating these events or even the chief protagonists to the whole of Israel's history. This is equivalent to the American schoolboy's ability to narrate George Washington's adventures with the axe and his ignorance of that man's place in presidential history.

It might help to compare, in a general way, the history of Israel with the history of the United States, realizing, of course, that there are vast differences between them. Americans celebrate the beginning of their independence from England with the signing of the Declaration of Independence in 1776 A.D. Israel celebrated its independence from Egypt with the acceptance of the covenant with God on Mount Sinai about 1280 B.C. (These things happened so long ago that we can give only approximate dates.)

Just as American history goes back a couple hundred years before the Declaration of Independence, so does Israel's history go back far beyond the exodus and covenant. The great patriarchs, Abraham, Isaac and Jacob, had lived between 1800 and 1700 B.C. Then, around 1700, Joseph and his brothers went down into Egypt where they and their descendants remained for some 400 years until the time of Moses and the exodus. Just how many people were involved in the descent into Egypt and in the later exodus is unknown. There were many elements of future Israel who did not experience the Egyptian captivity either personally or through their ancestors. They experienced it only in the cult which they accepted as the expression of their faith in the same God who had saved an actual people.

After the covenant on Mount Sinai and the declaration of

freedom, the Israelites wandered in the desert for close to forty years. Then, around 1250 B.C., they began the conquest of the land of Palestine, which was called Canaan then. The conquest was a slow and gradual affair. The Israelite tribes were united mainly by reason of their faith in the true God; they had no one political leader. Occasionally a military leader, called a "judge," would rise up, like Gideon or Samson, and deliver them for a while from their enemies. But this was not the normal situation.

This condition lasted for almost two hundred years. Then, when the Philistines, who had settled on the western shore about the same time that Israel was making its presence felt in the eastern part of the country, began to expand inland and even threatened for a time to annihilate the Israelites, the latter became convinced of the need of a king who would unite them in their battle against the common enemy. Despite religious objections on the ground that a human king would be a threat to the theocracy, Saul, the first king, was anointed. It was about 1020 B.C. After some twenty years of almost constant military operations, he died in battle and was succeeded by David. David, the most successful of Israel's kings, defeated all its enemies and extended the kingdom further than it had been or ever would be after him. In fact, Israel was now an empire. He united all the people under him, engaged in much building activity, made Jerusalem the political and religious center of the empire, and organized liturgical worship in a way that would help make Israel's faith in God a living reality. David reigned from 1000 to 961 B.C.

He was succeeded by his son, Solomon, who reigned from 961 to 922 B.C. A great builder and administrator, Solomon was responsible for strengthening much of the work done by his father. He built the great temple in Jerusalem, the capital, and brought much wealth and prosperity to the land. But the country was financially incapable of carrying the burden of all these building activities. Solomon was consequently forced to tax his people heavily and even to engage them in forced-labor projects. His popularity understandably waned considerably in the later years of his life. He would be held largely responsible for the schism that was to come.

After Solomon's death his son, Rehoboam, succeeded him and attempted to continue his father's ruinous policies. It was too much for the northern tribes who, in 922 B.C., rebelled against Judah, setting up their own king and forming their own nation. The event can be compared to the Civil War although the outcome was of a vastly different kind. From now on there were two kingdoms, that in the south being known as Judah while the general title of Israel was retained in the north. These, of course, were political names when used of the two kingdoms. The name "Israel" continued to be applied to all the people in a religious sense. The northern kingdom was much larger and had more people, but the southern kingdom had the natural political center of Jerusalem, the temple with the Ark of the Covenant and the dynasty of David reigning on the throne.

This period is, for obvious reasons, called the period of the divided kingdom. It was during this period that most of the great prophets lived and exercised their ministry. Some, like Elijah, Amos and Hosea, preached in the north; others, like Isaiah, Micah and Jeremiah, preached in the south. Both kingdoms belonged to God's chosen people, and both heard God's word spoken by His prophets. The northern kingdom lasted about 200 years, from 922 to 721 B.C., when it was destroyed by the Assyrians. Many of the people were taken into exile and lost their importance for sacred history. Others fled into the southern kingdom. Still others remained behind and intermarried with foreigners whom the Assyrians had brought into the land. The Samaritans of a later period were descended from this heterogeneous population.

The southern kingdom of Judah lasted almost 150 years longer. It was defeated by the Babylonians in 587 B.C. (Jeremiah and Ezekiel were both living at this time.) Jerusalem and the temple were destroyed and many of the people carried into exile in Babylon. But helped by the preaching of a couple of great prophets, these people in exile retained their religious convictions and their desire to return to their homeland. About forty years later the Babylonians were defeated by the Persians, whose king, Cyrus, permitted the Jewish exiles to return. This was in 538 B.C. Now began the work of reconstruction. The exile had had a great influence on the people; the problems of sin and suffering were discussed as never before. And the prophets of the period encouraged the people to repent of their past sins and to rebuild Jerusalem and the temple to the glory of God.

Less than a hundred years after the return from the exile in Babylon the prophetic office came to an end in Israel. Sent by God at various crises in the history of their people, the prophets accomplished their mission in a remarkable way. They kept alive Israel's unique faith in God and its hope in His final intervention for the world's salvation. More than 400 years would pass before that salvation would come in the person of Jesus Christ. But what the prophets had achieved in those 500 years between (approximately) 1000 and 500 B.C. would never be forgotten.

As we begin to study some of the specific achievements of the individual prophets it will be good to keep this general survey of Israel's history before us. Only in this way will we be able to see the picture in its proper perspective. Finally, the following dates and historical summaries are offered as convenient pegs around which can be grouped the particular historical facts that we shall meet.

B.C.	
1800–1700	Patriarchs (Abraham, Isaac, Jacob and family) in Canaan.
1700–1280	Hebrew people in Egypt.
1280–1250	Exodus, covenant, wandering in desert.
1250–1020	Conquest of Canaan and period of judges.
1020–922	Period of united monarchy (Saul, David, Solomon).
922–721	Period of northern kingdom (Israel).
922–587	Period of southern kingdom (Judah).
587–538	Exile in Babylon.
538–331	Period of Persian control.

3.

THREE NON-WRITING PROPHETS

NATHAN AND DAVID

It was about the year 1000 B.C. The fledgling kingdom of Israel was reeling under the heavy blows of an enemy army superior to it in weaponry and available manpower. Its very first king, Saul of the tribe of Benjamin, had just lost his life in battle on the mount of Gilboa. The great Samuel, first of the prophets and unifying spirit of the twelve tribes, was already dead. Israel was poised at the crossroads of history. The possibility of gradual annihilation was most real. The need for a vigorous leader to rouse the people to victory was never greater.

The believing Israelite had no doubt that a leader would be raised up. He knew that the Lord God had not brought them out of the land of Egypt with a strong hand and an outstretched arm for nothing. The divine plan must yet be accomplished. And Israel was the means of its accomplishment. Of this the faithful Israelite was convinced. Moreover, he had little difficulty in determining the particular instrument that God would choose. For there was a man named David of the tribe of Judah.

The signs of David's future greatness were abundant enough. A clear illustration of this is to be found in the sacred author's story about an event in David's early life. We read that Samuel, moved by the spirit of God, went down to Bethlehem to anoint the future king. After having been presented with the seven older sons of Jesse and having rejected them, Samuel was finally introduced to the young David who had been shepherding his father's flock in the fields. Immediately Samuel anointed him, "And the spirit of the Lord came upon David from that day forward" (1 Sam 16:13). In quick succession David gained the admiration and the confidence of his countrymen, of Jonathan, Saul's son, and of Saul himself. His exploits in battle became legendary (1 Sam 18:7), so legendary, in fact, that he later became the object of Saul's bitter jealousy. Finally he was forced to flee for his life, living first as an outlaw with a band of faithful retainers in the scrubby hills of Judah, and later as an outcast in the land of the Philistine enemy.

And here in Philistia he learned the news of Saul's death. David acted swiftly. Returning to his native land he was joyously welcomed by his kinsmen of Judah and anointed king of his own tribe. Then he set about to win the other tribes also. It was no easy matter. The tribe of Judah was not looked upon with the greatest of favor by the other tribes, especially those of the north. They preferred as king the one remaining son of Saul, a weak character named Ishbosheth. David, however, was equal to the occasion. By a remarkable show of human understanding he gained their good will and their agreement to accept him as king of all Israel. Anointed at the ancient town of Hebron, he immediately proved himself by taking the strategic city of Jerusalem, built high on one of the hills of Judah and until now still inhabited by its ancient Jebusite citizens. He made it the political capital of the now resurgent kingdom. Moreover, he went forth to do battle against the neighboring peoples who showed themselves inimical and to defeat them. The security of Israel was assured, at least for the time.

48

It was David's aim to make Jerusalem also the religious center of the kingdom. To this end he had the Ark of the Covenant, symbol of tribal unity and mystical dwelling place of God among His people, transported in solemn ceremony to the capital city. Nor was this enough. He decided, too, to build a temple worthy of the God who had done such great things for them. It is on this occasion that we meet the prophet Nathan for the first time. It was Nathan's God-assigned task to tell David that this was not the time for building a temple to the Lord. God would rather build *Himself* a "house," the house or dynasty of David. It was a momentous announcement the prophet made, fraught with meaning for the rest of Israel's history and for the history of all mankind. God would raise up a son to David who would also be, in a certain sense, God's own son: "I will be to him a father, and he shall be to me a son" (2 Sam 7:14). There would always be a king descended from David to rule over God's people and in God's name. This was the "house of David" that God had established for Himself.

This oracle of Nathan the prophet would be long remembered in Israel. On its basis was the royal Psalm 88 (89) composed, in which the hope is expressed for the continuation of David's dynasty. In this oracle do we find the roots of that tremendous hope that one day there would come from the house of David an eternal king, son of David, to rule God's people forever.

In this action of Nathan the prophet we can find another instance of that prophetic policy already noted in Samuel's day, and that would last as long as the monarchy lasted. That policy was one of advising the kings in matters of state. It is remarkable when we stop to think of it. Even among the ancient peoples, who more readily accepted religion's influence on politics than does our contemporary society, the behavior of Israel's prophets was unique. These men were no cringing sycophants, as the religious leaders of the pagan countries frequently were. They were men of God who spoke the word of God fearlessly. And what is more remarkable still, they were accepted as such. From king to lowly peasant, all respected God's spokesmen, at least in the sense that we read in *Ezekiel:* "But you shall say to them: Thus says the Lord God! And whether they heed or resist—for they are a rebellious house—they shall know that a prophet has been among them" (2:4-5).

This is forcefully brought home to us in another scene in which David and Nathan again play the principal roles. It was, presumably, some time after the incident reported above. David had gone on to ever greater victories, extending the boundaries of the kingdom beyond the traditional limits. Not only a strong kingdom, but even an incipient empire was emerging. It wasn't large by our standards, to be sure, but it commanded the respect of the neighboring peoples. It was during one of Israel's campaigns across the Jordan River that the incident took place. It was springtime, that time when kings go out to war. "But David remained in Jerusalem" (2 Sam 11:1). Attracted by the beauty of a woman in a house near the royal palace and abusing his power as king, he had Bathsheba brought to him and committed adultery with her. But this was not the end of it. Hearing that Bathsheba was with child by him and fearing the outcry when it would be discovered that the woman had a child while her husband was at war in David's own army, the king had the man placed in the thick of the battle where he would be sure to die. Thus it happened and so did David add murder to the crime of adultery.

It was at this point that Nathan again stood before the king, not to bring a divine word of promise now, but a word of denunciation and of punishment. He told the king a parable. It was about a rich man who had many flocks and a poor man who had but one lamb. A stranger visited the rich man one day and the latter took by force the single lamb of the poor man and prepared it for his guest. On hearing the story David became exceedingly angry and commanded that the wealthy man be punished. *"Thou art the man,"* cried Nathan, and then proceeded to describe his punishment. Coming to his senses, David could only bow low before this spokesman of God and acknowledge his guilt, "I have sinned against the Lord" (2 Sam 12:13).

It is this fearless stand before even the royal throne that marks the prophet of Israel as a unique being, a uniqueness acknowledged by the king in his humble confession of the charge. Isolated examples of such fearlessness may be found among the religious leaders of the pagan nations; it is a consistent pattern in Israel. It can only be explained adequately by the prophet's and the people's conviction of a supreme God with a moral will for good, good that must be accomplished.

ELIJAH, CHAMPION OF TRUTH

The next great prophetic figure to appear against the background of Old Testament history is Elijah. His very name would have indicated to his Hebrew contemporaries what his mission in life was to be. It meant "my God is Yahweh," that is, the God who showed Himself to be the Lord of all history and the special God of Israel, the God who revealed His name as "Yahweh," this is the God of Elijah. And Elijah was to fight all his life for the truth of that God. If Elijah could say that Yahweh was his

51

God, Yahweh could equally say that Elijah was His prophet.

Elijah exercised his office in the first half of the ninth century, that is, between the years 900 and 850 B.C. This was a hundred years after Nathan's time, the last prophet we considered. And much had happened in those hundred years. David had been succeeded by his son Solomon who had a brilliant reign but one that exhausted the resources of the people. In his desire to build great monuments and cities and fortifications, he had brought the kingdom almost to financial bankruptcy and the people to a point of rebellion. Indeed, on the death of Solomon and the accession of his son Rehoboam, the tribes of the north (and they were the more numerous by far) did rebel against the kingdom of Judah and the house of David. This was about 922 B.C. From now until the end there would be two kingdoms representing God's people, the kingdom of Judah in the south represented mainly by the tribe of Judah, and the kingdom of the north that was now known as "Israel." Both, however, retained Yahweh as their God, and God sent His prophetic messengers to both groups.

Despite its numerical and geographical superiority, the northern kingdom of Israel was at a distinct disadvantage both politically and religiously. Politically it had no stable dynasty that would continue to produce a ruler such as the Davidic dynasty in the south. This brought on a succession of dynasties and a lack of continuity that made the kingdom very weak at times. It lasted but 200 years.

Religiously it was at a disadvantage because the symbol of their religious unity, the Ark of the Covenant, was still in Solomon's temple in Jerusalem. Since the political leaders did not want their people to make pilgrimages to Jerusalem for fear they would develop a desire for political reunion, they established shrines in their own kingdom. Here they also set up golden calves which, like the Ark of the Covenant, were considered symbols of the presence of Yahweh among them. It was an unhappy choice because the pagan Canaanites (and there were still many of them, especially in the north) worshipped one of their main gods in the form of a bull. It would not take much for the two symbols, one Yahwistic and one pagan, to become confused, particularly in the eyes of the simple people.

But then something else happened which complicated this already bad religious situation. The seventh king on the northern throne was Ahab. For political and economic reasons he had married the daughter of the king of neighboring Tyre. The woman was a fanatical worshipper of the false god Baal, and she brought this worship with her to her new home in Israel. Her name was Jezebel. The influence of Jezebel was enormous. Many of the Israelites began to worship Baal either out of a hypocritical desire to please the queen, or out of simple ignorance. Even where the true worship of Yahweh was retained, pagan elements were often introduced; this is known as syncretism. It was evident that if Yahwism was to continue in the north, a vigorous religious leader was needed to bring a halt to the paganizing influences.

Elijah was the divine choice to provide the leadership. Coming from the wild countryside of Gilead and appearing as "a hairy man with a girdle of leather about his loins" (4 Kgs 1:8), he must have seemed strange indeed to the sophisticated inhabitants of Israel. But there was no mistaking his teachings. He worshipped Yahweh and would stand up to any Israelite who failed to worship the same God and worship Him without guile. We first

meet him shortly after Ahab takes the throne and marries
Jezebel. And we meet him executing divine justice on the sinful
kingdom; he announces to the king a prolonged drought
(3 Kgs 17:1). It was to be characteristic of his mission to oppose
the king. But behind it all he was opposing Jezebel and her
false religion; the king was only a weak instrument of his wife's
scheming. Two incidents above all bring out this opposition
between prophet and pagan queen.

The first is the "contest" between Elijah's God and Jezebel's
god on the top of Mount Carmel. A showdown was definitely
called for. Jezebel had succeeded in making many inroads in the
worship of Yahweh. Her "prophets" had gone out among the
villagers and called them to worship the same god the queen
worshipped. Many found it convenient to do so. The "troubler
of Israel," as Ahab called Elijah (3 Kgs 18:17), challenged the
king to bring the prophets of Baal to the top of Mount Carmel
and there to see, within the sight of all Israel, which God was
the true God. So it was done. Then Elijah invited the Baal
prophets to call on their god to see if he would manifest in any
way his acceptance of the sacrifice they had prepared for him.
Long and loud they cried, but there was no response; "there was
no voice heard, nor did anyone answer, nor regard them as they
prayed" (3 Kgs 18:29). Then came Elijah's turn. Pouring an
abundance of water around the sacrifice, he prayed to his God,
"Hear me, O Lord, hear me, that this people may learn that
thou art the Lord God and that thou hast turned their heart
again" (3 Kgs 18:37). Suddenly the fire of the Lord came down
from heaven and consumed the offerings and dried up the
waters. Yahweh, the true God, had won the day.

We must confess that the stories of both Elijah and Elisha

(whom we shall meet shortly) have undergone extensive elaboration in the course of their theological interpretation by ancient Israel. This elaboration itself, even beyond its theological significance, is indicative of the outstanding popularity of these two men of God and of the impression they made on their contemporaries. It still seems reasonable, however, to suppose some historical incident involving Elijah and the prophets of Baal which gave rise to the present form of the story. This incident, whatever the details may have been, did much to restore the faith of many in Yahweh. But it also greatly enraged Jezebel. We read that Elijah was forced to flee because of her rage. He went far to the south and there experienced an encounter with God that is of some importance. We read that, as he stood on the sacred mount, there came by in succession a strong wind, an earthquake and a fire; but the Lord was in none of these. Then came the "whistling of a gentle air" (3 Kgs 19:11–13), and Elijah, recognizing the presence of God, covered his face with his mantle. The lesson that is being taught in this story, and which our prophet was one of the first in Israel to recognize, is that God's special presence is not to be sought necessarily in the great events of history, in those which are wrought with great éclat in the sight of men, but more often in the small and seemingly insignificant affairs of life. This might seem familiar spirituality to us of the twentieth Christian century. But for the period of ancient Israel it was a remarkable spiritualization of religion. No other ancient people had such a pervasive concept of their god. It is one more area where our spiritual heritage finds its roots in Old Testament religious convictions.

One more incident in Elijah's life that we must note is his confrontation with Ahab and Jezebel over the matter of Naboth's vineyard. This Israelite possessed a piece of land greatly desired by the king. When the man refused to sell it to him, Jezebel then had Naboth unjustly accused of blasphemy and put to death. And so did the vineyard pass over to the king without opposition. Such a blatant act of injustice could not go unnoticed. And Elijah was the man to notice it. Coming down upon Ahab and Jezebel in the fury of his wrath, he pronounced the divine words of punishment upon them. And to Jezebel in particular he said, "In this place, wherein the dogs have licked the blood of Naboth, they shall lick thy blood also" (3 Kgs 21:19).

We have had only a glimpse of this prophet. But we have seen enough to understand why later Israel would develop so much theology around him. Even in the earlier period his popularity is attested by the many stories that came to be told about him. These have been used by our inspired writer because they bring out so well the mighty power of Elijah's God, or because they teach the lessons of divine justice and divine truth that the prophet himself taught. And these, after all, are the really important matters in the story of Elijah.

ELISHA, GOD'S WONDER-WORKER

The story of Elijah's last day on earth is as filled with mystery as is the rest of his life. We read that, as he was walking with his younger companion and fellow prophet, Elisha, a fiery chariot appeared and Elijah "went up by a whirlwind into heaven" (4 Kgs 2:11). We cannot know now all that this meant to the original readers of the story; they would be much more familiar with the imagery contained in it. But we do know that later Israel looked upon it as a sign of Elijah's special place in the

56

whole great plan of salvation. So great was it, in fact, that the prophet Malachi much later was to declare that the great day of the Lord would be prepared by an Elijah (Mal 3:23). And Jesus himself was to assure his followers that John the Baptist had fulfilled that role (Mk 9:10–12). The prophet had left an indelible mark on salvation history.

But we are interested here in the companion of Elijah's last days. It is the same Elisha who witnessed the mysterious passing of the great prophet. It is this Elisha who received the mantle of his predecessor, signifying his continuation of the prophetic work. Elisha appears as quite a different person than Elijah. While the latter was dour and ascetic and fled the company of his fellow men except when God's business called him, Elisha was beloved by all and was almost always seen in the company of others. A woman of Sunam probably expressed the conviction of most Israelites when she said, "I perceive that this is a holy man of God, who often passeth by us" (4 Kgs 4:9). The divine choice of these two completely different persons can be explained readily enough. The outright idolatry of Elijah's time needed the forbidding figure of a prophet of wrath and of doom. Once the battle for Yahweh had been won, (or at least His opponents routed for the time; the battle was never fully won) God chose a gentler figure to mirror His own mercy on a repentant people.

This divine mercy was especially reflected in the miracle stories surrounding Elisha. The difference in this respect between Elijah and Elisha is again remarkable. Few stories are told of Elijah's wonder-working but those that are told are spectacular in nature and are designed to manifest, in no unmistakable way to a people whose hearts had been hardened, the divine anger because of sin. The long drought that sorely afflicted the people of the north was seen as God's reaction to sin; the awe-inspiring and fiery consumption of the sacrifice on Mount Carmel proclaimed mightily His incontestable right to the adoration of His people. While many more stories were told of Elisha, they are less cataclysmic in nature and more expressive of God's loving concern for His people. The giving of life to the dead, the cleansing of lepers of their disease, the bringing of food to the hungry—all these are attributed to Elisha. As we have already mentioned, it is impossible now to reconstruct the precise historical nature of all these actions. What we can be sure of is that our inspired author has used these stories to emphasize the divine mercy. It was divine mercy that marked the age of Elisha, just as it had been the divine wrath that had marked the age of Elijah.

A word might be said here about the role of miracles in salvation history, for there is always the danger, frequently succumbed to, of attaching undue importance to them. The ancient Israelites (and all biblical writers for that matter) had no concept of a miracle as we do, a concept based on philosophical analysis. For them every event in history and every phenomenon of nature was an instance of the immediate work of God. I believe it was Chesterton who put it best when he described the ancient Israelite's picture of God's daily command to the sun, "get up and do it again." Those events or those phenomena which Israel saw as particularly significant for the unfolding of sacred history she called, quite appropriately, "signs and wonders." In the inspired description of these signs and wonders, the "sign" or "wonder" element would be emphasized in order to indicate the message for the faithful reader. In the light of this mentality, which could be strikingly illustrated by different authors' interpretations of the same "sign" or "wonder," it is obvious that it is most difficult to determine when a miracle in our sense of the word is involved. It is best, therefore, to accept that meaning of the story which the sacred author intended, convinced that that meaning was sufficiently based in historical events to be recognized by the man of God and by his faithful hearers.

Another characteristic of Elijah's successor was his interest in the "sons of the prophets." We saw when we studied the beginnings of prophecy in Israel that the first prophets went about in bands, attracting similar-minded young men to them. We find such groups now in Elisha's time. They lived in communities and went about preaching the true religion. As we have seen, the great prophets like Nathan and Elijah were not closely associated with these groups; they seemed to have received a special vocation not granted to the "sons of the prophets." Elisha, on the other hand, while he stood out by reason of his activity, seemingly considered himself one of the community. Doubtless his presence among them helped to strengthen their position among the people and make them more acceptable.

Like almost all the prophets, Elisha took an active part in the political life of Israel. We can recall that involvement in political affairs was almost essential to the prophetic office. This was because of the peculiar make-up of the Israelite state. It was conceived of as an instrument used by God for the governing of His special people. The kings were anointed in a religious rite and the spirit of God was considered to be in them. They were expected by their office to promote the worship of Yahweh and to wipe out all traces of idolatry. It is no wonder, then, that the prophets took a great interest in the kings and in the social and political life of their times. Elisha was no exception; he, too, was a man involved.

Our prophet inherited the situation left him by Elijah. Although the cause of Yahweh had triumphed through the victory of Mount Carmel, the pagan queen Jezebel was still alive, and Ahab's son, Joram, was reigning as king. Elisha must have inherited also a great fear of the dangers that this ruling family could bring to the true religion. At any rate, we find him taking it upon himself to anoint a new king of Israel. It was when Israel was at war against the neighboring Syrians. Joram at the time was back at his palace recovering from a wound received in battle. Elisha seized the opportunity to send a messenger to the battlefield to anoint one of the officers of the army as the new king of Israel (see 4 Kgs 9).

After his anointing, Jehu, the new king, initiated a bloody reform whose dimensions surely were not fully foreseen by Elisha. First he had the king, Joram, and Jezebel, the queen mother, put to death, fulfilling the prophecy made by Elijah some years before. Then he wiped out the entire royal family, thus assuring that no one of them would claim the throne. Finally he had all the false prophets of Baal brought together and had them all brutally murdered. It was not a glorious page in the history of Israel; almost a hundred years later the prophet Hosea would look back upon it and see it as a crime that needed divine vengeance (Hos 1:4). We are a bit shocked by these instances of cruelty and even more so by the association, whatever its extent might have been, of God's prophets with them. But we must be aware—and the Old Testament provides us with sufficient examples to establish that awareness—that in the evolving of salvation history God does not change radically and without human response the instrument He is working with. Any changes will always be commensurate with man's response to the divine action. If He chooses, therefore, to make use of the imperfect institutions and imperfect human beings of a primitive society, we should wonder only at the patience of such a God and at His infinite wisdom that knows how to lead these to the fullness of revelation.

Despite the cruelty, the brutality and the primitiveness of that history, the figure of Elisha stands out as a symbol of the divine mercy that will never be wanting. As such he prefigured another wonder-worker, another Prophet who would come "with the Holy Spirit and with power," and who would go about "doing good and healing all who were in the power of the devil, for God was with him" (Acts 10:38).

4.

AMOS, HOSEA, MICAH

AMOS, SHEPHERD AND PROPHET

ON the death of Solomon the northern tribes had broken away from the house of David. "Israel" now existed as a separate, political unity, although the name continued to be applied to all the people in a religious sense. A succession of weak or mediocre kings seemed to threaten an early end for the kingdom of the north. Then came Omri (876–869 B.C.), a powerful ruler who let his neighbors know that Israel was far from dead. To him and to his successors the nation owed the continuation of its independence and influence. It was under Omri's son, Ahab, as we saw, that paganism became a real threat to the people. It was such a danger that God saw fit to raise up an Elijah and an Elisha to cope with it. Their success was not absolute. Almost a hundred years later, under another king of another dynasty, another danger threatened to engulf the people. And again God called on His spokesman to bring the word to His people. The spokesman was Amos, shepherd of Judah.

The northern kingdom had developed considerably over the years. Now under Jeroboam II, who ruled from 786 to 746 B.C., prosperity had arrived. Israel had gained control of much land on the other side of the Jordan, and Damascus, her frequent enemy of the past, had just been severely defeated by the slowly awakening giant, Assyria, who, however, had been unable to follow up its victory at the time. This left Israel free to grow and expand and become fat with success. Unfortunately, the success was tainted. It had been achieved at the expense of social justice. The rich were taking advantage of the poor, the merchants were cheating their customers, even the judges were giving false decisions. Wealth had sapped the nation of a sense of the right. But this was not all. It had made them soft and weak, prone to laxness in all those virtues that make a people and a nation strong and enduring. And this general deterioration of morality inevitably influenced their liturgical worship of the true God.

All of this we know from the prophet Amos. And a thoroughly unique messenger this man of God was. He came from Tekoa, a village in the hills of Judah to the south. Most of Amos's working day was spent outside the village in the scrubby hills and sun-baked valleys of Judah, where he led his flocks to whatever pasture there was. Here in the overwhelming solitude of this wilderness he felt the presence of God in a way his ancestors once had when they staggered through the wilderness of Sinai towards the Land of Promise. The God of Amos was, of course, the God of all the people. But the shepherd of Tekoa saw aspects of this God that others failed to see at times. True, He was a God who loved His people; His saving actions were proof enough of that. But Amos saw Him also as a sternly moral God, a God whom nature obeyed with undeviating regularity. When a lion seizes its prey, it *always* roars by reason of its God-given nature (3:4). And oxen cannot be used to plow the sea (6:12).

In his shepherd's life Amos had much time to think about God, to contemplate His majesty as revealed in the harshly beau-

63

tiful landscape about him. Here, too, he became increasingly conscious of the pervading presence of God, of His interest in and concern for the most insignificant detail. Here, too, Amos heard God telling him one day to go to the neighboring kingdom of Israel in the north and take a message of woe. A strange affair! A man from Judah, and a sunburned, mirthless shepherd at that, is asked to bring God's word to a sophisticated, prosperous people of another kingdom. But God's ways are not men's ways. He chooses His messengers to suit His message, and this message was a stern and mirthless one.

That Amos was even able to utter the first words in the busy streets of Bethel may be difficult to conceive. Wouldn't these gaily dressed citizens give this rough creature a glance and then hurry on? Would even the poor and the beggars—and there were enough of these—be interested in one who supposedly brought God's message from afar, since their own town of Bethel was itself a religious center whose fame went back hundreds of years? But for all their sophistication and self-sufficiency it must be said that these people were aware of the unpredictable ways of their God. At times they could recognize His messengers even in the most humble of garb. Moreover, Amos's first words were sweet to the ears of Israel. He began by condemning all of their neighbors: Damascus, Philistia, Tyre, Edom, Ammon, Moab and even Judah (1:3–2:5). Now here was a prophet who made sense! But then, just as they were beginning to enjoy to the full this herdsman's harsh words about their enemies, he suddenly turned on them. They, too, are included in the list of criminals! They are no better than their enemies in God's sight! Amos checks off their crimes as they listen in stunned silence, and the list makes clear that if justice is a mark of Yahweh's religion, this people is none of Yahweh's:

64

Thus says the Lord: For three crimes of Israel, and for four, I will not revoke my word; because they sell the just man for silver, and the poor man for a pair of sandals. They trample the heads of the weak into the dust of the earth, and force the lowly out of the way. Son and father go to the same prostitute, profaning my holy name. Upon garments taken in pledge they recline beside any altar; and the wine of those who have been fined they drink in the house of their god (2:6-8).

For Amos, accustomed to the relentless regularity of nature, justice could be defined as "that which must be." When the lion roars, man is afraid (3:8); it is the way of things. Justice is the proportion that must exist between the measure and the measured. When the wall is not in line with the plummet, then it is not straight, it is not "just." In human affairs, the measure is God's moral will. That is the plummet with which man's actions must be in line. If they are not, there is no justice (7:7-9). Israel had a special reason to practice justice. God had revealed His moral will to her; she knew it as no other people knew it. There was no excuse of ignorance for her. Moreover, God had given Israel reason enough to follow that will. Had He not brought her up from the land of Egypt, led her through the desert for forty years and given her the land to occupy (2:10)? Israel would be hard put to it to justify her present ways.

One of the more striking passages in the book is a scathing denunciation of the women of Samaria:

Hear this word, women of the mountain of Samaria, you cows of Bashan, you who oppress the weak and abuse the needy; who say to your lords, "Bring drink for us!" The Lord God has sworn by his holiness: Truly the days are coming upon you when they shall drag you away with hooks, the last of you with fishhooks; you shall go out through the breached walls each by the most direct way, and you shall be cast into the mire, says the Lord (4:1-3).

65

Amos, it must be insisted, was no misogynist. If his biting criti-
cism of the other elements of Israelite society stemmed basically
from a deep concern for Israel, then his words against the
women must not be interpreted as anti-feminist jargon. Indeed,
it is only among a people that respects the dignity of woman-
hood that horror over woman's degradation can be manifested.
No similar horror is to be found in pagan literature. There
woman is pictured, even in a deified form, as ordered to abuse
by nature. Israel, on the other hand, knew that her God had
entered into dialogue with women just as with men, as the cases
of Sarah, Miriam, Deborah and others bore witness. Woman,
therefore, must share the same dignity as man since she shares
that which is most constitutive of that dignity, the possibility of
colloquy with the divine. The Yahwist author, in his highly
stylized story of woman's creation and of the fall, gives what is
for that ancient period startling witness of this conviction. Amos,
we can rightly argue, was no less convinced, even though his
identification of the luxury-loving ladies of Samaria with the fat
cows of Bashan strikes a jarring note on our ears. Isaiah, as we
shall see, was no less harsh in his incrimination of female vanity.

The prophet of Tekoa had another charge to lay before these
people. In a sense it was harder to take than the one he had already made. It concerned their understanding of God's future
plans for His people. It was an almost necessary element of the
Hebrew religion that God, who had intervened in history in the
past to save His people, would intervene again in the future to
bring salvation to its climax. The precise manner and other
details of this intervention were only gradually unfolded in the
course of Israel's long history. Also, whether this intervention was
understand, in the period before the exile, to mark a new period of
history is not at all certain. The exile would do much to sharpen

66

Israel's focus in these matters. By Amos's time, in the eighth century B.C., there was at least the conviction that God would come one day. Moreover, they were convinced that He would come to destroy all their enemies and to give His people perfect peace. This would be the "day of the Lord" to which they looked forward with much keen anticipation. But again Amos frustrates this most basic of hopes. "Woe to those" he cries, "who yearn for the day of the Lord! What will this day of the Lord mean for you? Darkness and not light!" (5:18).

Israel had perverted the very meaning of the covenant that God had made with her. And the people of the north had had ample opportunity to reflect on that meaning since, as the scholars have shown, much of the rich theology of the covenant, as presented, for example, in the Elohistic and Deuteronomistic traditions in the Pentateuch, can be traced back to the northern kingdom. According to this theology the covenant, with its stipulations binding Israel, was the expected response of a people that had been saved by the mighty acts of its God. The Commandments were an expression of Israel's loyalty to the saving, moral God. God's continuing protection was implicitly conditioned by His people's response. That response, in Amos's time, was not being made. And the prophet warns them that, just as they had once met God in the wilderness years ago, they should prepare to meet Him again, but the meeting will not be one of salvation but of judgment (4:12–13).

The climax of Amos's ministry seems to have been his meeting with the priest of Bethel. The occasion was a "word" that the prophet had uttered against the royal house. Speaking in God's name he had said, "I will attack the house of Jeroboam with the sword" (7:9). Amaziah, the priest, immediately gave it political dimensions. Amos was guilty of treason (7:10–11)! Whether or not Amaziah really thought this, he was probably most uneasy about the prophet's presence and sought any excuse to get rid of him. Confronting the herdsman of Tekoa in the streets of Bethel, Amaziah charges him in these words, "Off with you, visionary, flee to the land of Juda! There earn your bread by prophesying . . ." (7:12). It is easy to imagine the prophet's indignation in the face of this accusation. He, Amos, prophesying to earn bread! "I was no prophet, nor have I belonged to a company of prophets," he cried (7:14). In other words, he did not come here on his own, to make a living. He was living a peaceful life as a herdsman when God called him (7:15–16). "The Lord God speaks—who will not prophesy!" (3:8). No human force, be he priest or king, would keep this man of God from his appointed vocation.

Amos exploded in Israel like a mighty force. His strong cry for justice, for concern for the poor, still has meaning for today. Here was a strong, stolid, stern champion of God's among a people weak, soft and pampered. They needed a man like Amos, and God sent him to them. It is interesting that this rough shepherd of Tekoa should be the first of the great writing prophets, the first to leave a record of his oracles for posterity. Other prophets after him would fill out the picture of an almost unrelieved sense of doom left by Amos. But Amos had a mission to fulfill and he fulfilled it. We can still learn from him.

HOSEA, PROPHET OF DIVINE LOVE

Amos and Hosea both prophesied in the northern kingdom. Both were active during the reign of Jeroboam II (787–746 b.c.). But there is no evidence that the one knew the other. The similarity between the two lies almost solely in the situation they faced and in the God whose word they spoke. Other than this, Amos and Hosea are as different as two prophets can be. It is as though a particular period of history were being held up like a giant mirror before the divine will. Held one way, it reflects the picture of stern, unbending justice. Held another way, it casts an image of anguished, unrequited love.

No doubt the differing backgrounds of the two had much to do with their differing outlook. For one thing, Amos was not a native of the northern kingdom, and Hosea was. The former, therefore, could condemn these crimes with less emotion; the natural ties were less binding. Also, nature's harshness in the wild hills of Judah left its mark on the shepherd of Tekoa. Hosea had no such background. One thing suffices to understand Hosea. It is his personal life, a life that mirrored so perfectly the life of Israel with God that God made use of it to make perfectly clear to His people what they had done to Him. For Hosea was married to a prostitute, a woman who loved other men and gave herself to them. It is difficult to tell whether Hosea's wife was actually a prostitute when he married her, or whether she became one only after the marriage. At any rate, the symbolism would remain the same. Gomer, Hosea's wife, was just like Israel whom God had taken to Himself as His bride, but who now rejected His love and sought other gods. Israel was guilty of spiritual adultery.

We must try to imagine the anguish in the prophet's soul as he thought of Israel's infidelity. He could picture to himself perfectly the divine emotions, and he describes them as he would his own. For Yahweh and he had shared the same experience; both had unfaithful lovers! This is a bold figure, to be sure, and is even a bit startling to our modern Western minds. We feel ill at ease with such imagery. Our cultural tradition and our whole mentality abhor the more vivid anthropomorphisms when speaking of God. We speak more freely of His omnipotence, His omniscience or the infinity of His love. These abstract concepts, the products of our analytical minds, were completely foreign to the ancient Hebrews. The vivid, the concrete, the tangible—these alone were they able to grasp. While we might claim a greater sophistication for our manner of speaking of the divine, we must take seriously this other manner which even the Son of God chose to adopt in His dealings with His fellow men.

The Israelites, then, of Hosea's time were told that they were no better than common prostitutes. By this the prophet meant not only that some worshipped the pagan gods, but also that others introduced pagan practices into the worship of the true God. Thus the people of the northern kingdom used the statue of a golden calf which was worshipped by many as God Himself. Hosea cries out in disgust, "The work of an artisan, no god at all, destined for the flames—such is the calf of Samaria!" (8:6). This false worship (called "idolatry" when it is the worship of false gods, and "syncretism" when it is the worship of the true God in pagan ways) was also accompanied by all manner of vice. Hosea condemns them for this, too, for injustice and immorality, for drunkenness, lying and murder:

Hear the word of the Lord, O people of Israel, for the Lord has a grievance against the inhabitants of the land: There is no fidelity, no mercy, no knowledge of God in the land. False swearing, lying, murder, stealing and adultery! in their lawlessness, bloodshed follows bloodshed (4:1–2).

In a special way does he blame the leaders for this situation, the priests and kings and false prophets (4:4–5:7). In their own abandonment of God's law they have carried the whole nation

70

with them to the brink of disaster. In the prophet's portrayal of this we get a better appreciation of the need for worthy leaders.

All of these crimes were direct violations of the law given them by God. The law was, in a sense, part of the marriage contract between Israel and Yahweh. The latter had sealed a covenant between the two. While the covenant was bilateral, involving both parties in some way, it was not between equals. Therefore, the common element of the covenant—Hosea called it *ḥesed* in Hebrew, which we can translate for the moment as covenant love—was not to be understood in precisely the same way of Yahweh and Israel. For Yahweh *ḥesed* was expressed in His steadfast loving kindness to His people, in His saving actions; we could translate it in this case as grace, not in the technical sense of the scholastics, but in the biblical sense of a free favor granted by God in love. On Israel's part *ḥesed* was the response of loyalty to this grace, a response manifested in the observation of Yahweh's moral will. It is this *ḥesed,* therefore, that Israel violates every time she fails to observe the moral will of God. She is being disloyal to the one who has been supremely loyal to her. Hosea is able to describe this disloyalty so vividly because he has experienced it in his own life.

The prophet, on God's command, carries his symbolism even further. He has three children by Gomer and each is given a name that will have special meaning for Israel. The first child is called Jezreel (1:3-5), the name of a valley in Israel where a bloody massacre had taken place (see 2 Kings 9–10); the name would remind Israel of this awful event in her history, of one of the more execrable examples of her violation of *ḥesed*. The second child is called "Unloved" or "Unpitied," and the third child "Not-my-people." The meaning of these names would be clear to all who heard them, for they pointed to Israel. Again, all of this seems very strange to us. But the ancient peoples were much addicted to symbolic names. And the names that Hosea gave his children would take on added significance because of the context of the prophet's ministry. Moreover, because he *was* a prophet, what he did would be quickly noised about. Israel's character was being vividly delineated in the names of these children; she would not be slow to grasp this.

There is a theme that is found in Hosea that will appear in other prophets, too. It is another one of Israel's weaknesses in the prophet's eyes. This is the desire to form military alliances with foreign powers. We are in the world of politics here and it is not always clear, from a natural viewpoint, why an alliance with a stronger power would not be the better policy. It is a problem we'll face frequently in the prophets. At the time of Hosea, both Assyria and Egypt were growing in power. It is not too difficult to understand why a smaller kingdom like Israel should seek the help of one of these. But for the prophets these nations are the worshippers of false gods and are therefore unworthy of being linked in any way with Israel. Moreover, and this is even more to the point, Israel has Yahweh! If she would put her trust in Him as she should, she would not have to call upon Egypt and Assyria "like a dove, silly and senseless" (7:11). Yahweh is the supreme Lord of history, and Israel must have absolute confidence in Him.

There is no evidence that Hosea was around when the policy he condemned reached its predicted climax. After the death of Jeroboam II, Israel was ruled by a succession of six kings within a period of twenty years; none of them died a natural death. It was a period of increasing tension within Israel, different factions striving for control. One faction favored an alliance with Assyria, the other with Egypt. None was content to rely totally on Yahweh. This internal division and growing secularization were finally climaxed by the destruction of the northern kingdom at the hands of the Assyrian army in 721 B.C. Hosea had expressed it in this way: "Because you have trusted in your chariots, and in your many warriors, turmoil shall break out among your tribes and all your fortresses shall be ravaged as Salman ravaged Beth-Arbel in time of war, smashing mothers and their children. So shall it be done to you, Bethel, because of your utter wickedness; at dawn the king of Israel shall perish utterly" (10:13-15). In attributing their downfall to the failure to trust in Yahweh, Hosea speaks from the conviction of faith, a conviction that goes deeper than that formed by natural arguments but which does not for that reason contradict the latter.

Before we close our study of the northern kingdom, it will be helpful to take a quick glance at the political setup once again. It will help us to appreciate the differing views taken by the prophets of the north and of the south and of the consequent enrichment of revelation. Throughout her existence as an independent nation, Israel was governed by a succession of dynasties. Unlike in Judah, where the dynasty of David prevailed until the end, there was no political stability in Israel. This was partly conditioned by, and at the same time, served to confirm, the conviction that God was the only ruler of Israel. Led by this conviction, the people would think little of deposing a human ruler. And if God did want a particular individual to act as king, He would indicate His choice in some special way, as He had with the judges in the past. The charismatic rather than the dynastic ruler was the ideal of the north. Hosea wasn't too happy with human kingship. He had seen its abuses and the failure of rulers to bring real peace. Above all, he considered it an infringement on the divine rights. "They made kings, but not by my authority," he says in the name of the Lord, "they established princes, but without my approval" (8:4). Again speaking in God's name he tells them, "I give you a king in my anger, and I take him away in my wrath" (13:11).

But the real heart of our prophet's message is the unquenchable love of God for His people. Just as Hosea was forced to take away from his faithless wife all the gifts he had bestowed upon her in the past in order to bring her to her senses (2:4–5.10–12), so would God take away from Israel all the signs of His favor:

> I will bring an end to all her joy, her feasts, her new moons, her Sabbaths and all her solemnities. I will lay waste her vines and fig trees, of which she said, "These are the hire my lovers have given me"; I will turn them into rank growth and wild beasts shall devour them. I will punish her for the days of the Baals, for whom she burnt incense while she decked herself out with her rings and her jewels, and, in going after her lovers, forgot me, says the Lord (2:13–15).

"Then she [Gomer and Israel] shall say, 'I will go back to my first husband, for it was better with me then than now'" (2:9). God could not destroy Israel completely. His love was too great for that. One of the most moving pieces in all of the literature of the Old Testament is the divine soliloquy in chapter 11, where Yahweh ponders the fate of His people. Their faithlessness deserves annihilation. But how can He who raised Israel as an only son destroy him now? He is God and not man! He *will* redeem His people! The change of figures note here from that of husband to that of father and from that of wife to that of son shows that Hosea wanted to exhaust all the expressions of human love to describe the divine love.

74

Here is the great difference between Amos and Hosea. The former predicted doom, but did not bother to state explicitly that this punishment was intended to make Israel repent. Hosea, overwhelmed by the divine love, sees and emphasizes the medicinal character of punishment. Yahweh will restore His bride one day to her rightful place, since the punishment meted out to the faithless lover is designed to bring her to her senses. This figure of divine love presented in the form of married love will be taken up again by other prophets and other sacred writers, even by Our Lord Himself. It was destined to become a classic figure in biblical revelation.

MICAH OF MORESHETH, PROPHET OF THE POOR

We leave the northern kingdom of Israel to its grim fate and pass on down to the southern kingdom of Judah. Here, too, God was to raise up His messengers who would bring the word to His people. In fact, of the great writing prophets, Judah was to produce a disproportionately large number. Isaiah, Jeremiah, Ezekiel are among the better known. These and others would make their contributions to Old Testament revelation and to God's gradually unfolding plan for man's salvation.

In Judah we find ourselves in an atmosphere that is not entirely unfamiliar. We recognize the same type of people as in the north, expressing themselves in the same language and with the same thought patterns, worshipping the same God in more or less the same way. We can even recognize some of the same failings: the tendency to incorporate pagan elements in their religious worship, crimes against social justice and sexual moral-

75

ity, and the itch to attain political security by foreign alliances. But there were also notable differences here. For one thing, the magnificent Temple of Jerusalem had no equal in the north. Here the liturgy was carried out with a splendor that was truly impressive. You can almost feel the pride of the people in this great building and in its services. It is easy to see how they could develop superstitious convictions concerning this Temple. It would be the object of many a prophetic oracle throughout its existence. Another important difference was on the political level. Where political instability was the order of the day throughout much of northern Israel's history, here in Judah a measure of stability was assured by the continuation of the Davidic dynasty. As we saw when we studied David and the prophet Nathan, God had promised Judah a king from the house of David as long as the kingdom lasted. Throughout the period of Judah's existence as an independent nation, from 922 to 587 B.C., this promise was fulfilled. The importance of this Davidic kingship would be reflected in many of the prophetic oracles.

We cannot here review all the history of Judah from the time of the split in 922 B.C. We are interested in the period in which the prophets play their role. And that period begins in the latter part of the eighth century B.C., that is, shortly after the period of Amos and Hosea in the north. In Judah the period is marked by the reigns of Jotham (742–735), Ahaz (735–715) and Hezekiah (715–687). As in the north, so in Judah there was relative peace and prosperity during the first part of this period. But the reigns of Ahaz and Hezekiah witnessed the rapidly swelling power of Assyria and the growth of its ambitions to win the west. Judah's life was to be greatly affected by this phenomenon.

Taking our attention away from this world scene, let us con-

sider the activities of a man who was much more concerned
with the fortunes of other men-in-the-street like himself than he
was with international politics. The man's name is Micah; he
comes from a village called Moresheth in the gently rolling foot-
hills of the Judean mountains to the west of Jerusalem. It is
sufficiently distant from Jerusalem not to be affected by every
rumor or every incident that stirs the capital city. Micah became,
by God's grace and in a manner known to him alone, God's
prophet.

What we have just said about Moresheth is not to be understood in the sense that Micah had no knowledge of outside events
or that he made no reference to them in his oracles. In fact, the
point of departure for his prophecies is the holy Temple of
Jerusalem:

Hear, O peoples, all of you, give heed, O earth, and all that fills you!
Let the Lord God be witness against you, the Lord from his holy
temple! For see, the Lord comes forth from his place, he descends
and treads upon the heights of the earth (1:2–3).

The Lord will appear here in a special way and bring judgment
against His people. Samaria, the capital of the northern kingdom,
and Jerusalem, the capital of Judah, are named as the responsible
agents for all the crimes of the people (1:5). Their punishment is
sure and all will feel its effects (1:6–16). The reference to the
northern kingdom shows that Micah began his ministry before
that kingdom's collapse in 721 B.C. Also, note that he refers to her
as a harlot (1:7), a figure that Hosea had already applied to
her shortly before this. Note, too, that the prophet of Moresheth
castigates the northern kingdom for its religious crimes (note the
"idols" in 1:7). These similarities naturally lead scholars to
speculate on the question of literary dependence. There seems

77

little doubt that Hosea would have expressed these concepts before Micah and, therefore, that the latter would have been dependent on the former. Even here, there are varying possibilities. Micah may have been acquainted with the expressions when he actually delivered the oracles in oral form, or he may have used them only in the later literary redaction.

But when he comes to the southern kingdom Micah has a different kind of crime to emphasize. It is the oppression of the poor by the rich. We are reminded of Amos's outbursts against the wealthy people of Israel. Micah is even more outspoken, if that is possible, about social injustice in Judah. The rich are gradually monopolizing the land and homes of the poor by exacting pledges from them that they are unable to pay (2:10). In this way they even succeed in taking over property that had been in the family for generations. Such property was considered inviolate among God's people (see 1 Kgs 21:1–4); but the greed of the rich made them forget these ideals. Social injustice is always a serious crime. The situation becomes much more serious when the leaders of the people close their eyes to the injustices and even accept bribes to overlook them. Micah makes this accusation, and in a scathing passage he vividly pictures what they are doing to the poor:

And I said: Hear, you leaders of Jacob, rulers of the house of Israel! Is it not your duty to know what is right, you who hate what is good, and love evil? You who tear their skin from them, and their flesh from their bones! They eat the flesh of my people, and flay their skin from them, and break bones. They chop them in pieces like flesh in a kettle, and like meat in a caldron (3:1–3).

There are false prophets, too, who brazenly further these injustices by their own venal character (3:5).

To all of this Micah can only see one end. He had already predicted the collapse of Samaria; Jerusalem will suffer the same fate:

Therefore, because of you, Sion shall be plowed like a field, and Jerusalem reduced to rubble, and the mount of the temple to a forest ridge (3:12).

If he delivered this oracle in the capital city itself, we can imagine the horrified reaction. Jerusalem was the place where God dwelled in a special way. It was inviolable, and everyone knew it. Yet this farmer from Moresheth had the audacity to say that Jerusalem would be "reduced to rubble, and the mount of the temple to a forest ridge." It took courage to say those words, courage and a deep faith that had engendered strong convictions. This is the courage and this the faith that distinguished the true prophets of the Old Testament. No other people ever produced a class of men like them.

It is another characteristic of Israel's prophets that they were not so overwhelmed by the sins of the people that they forgot entirely about the divine will to save. That is why, almost invariably, we find interspersed with the prophecies of doom other oracles about future redemption. God's plan cannot be totally vitiated. Hosea, as we saw, had pictured God restoring His faithless bride. And the post-exilic editor of the oracles of Amos could not conclude the book with a picture of destruction (Am 9:8). He added the messianic epilogue (9:9–15) which is necessary to do full justice to God's nature. The picture of restoration is understandably vague at first. But as prophet follows prophet, the picture takes on more and more detail. It never, of course, comes close to depicting the full reality as it was manifested in the New Testament period. But enough is there at the end for the man of faith to see the fulfillment as an organic continuation of the prophetic revelation.

Hosea had simply foreseen the restoration. Micah connects the restoration with a special ruler of Judah who will come forth from Bethlehem:

But you, Bethlehem-Ephratha, too small to be among the clans of Juda, from you shall come forth for me one who is to be ruler in Israel; whose origin is from of old, from ancient times (5:1).

This, we know, was perfectly fulfilled by the birth of Jesus (Matt 2:6). But it required no special divine insight on Micah's part to point to Bethlehem as the birthplace of the messianic ruler. As the descendant par excellence of the great David, He would necessarily be described as coming forth from the place of David's origin. It is simply a way of saying that he would be another David. Micah is casting his oracle in the context of the history of his own people.

This is one of the earliest references to the future Davidic ruler who would save his people. The reference would have come most naturally, of course, from a prophet of Judah who was heir to all that had been said about David in the past. The reference does not necessarily indicate a strictly eschatological event, one representing a divine intervention ushering in a new era. It is, however, of importance in the gradually developing messianism of the Old Testament revelation. It should be noted that the oracle falls quite readily in place in the prophet's development of his address to his people. It is, unfortunately, like many other messianic passages, taken frequently from its context and studied in an historical vacuum. The process leads inevitably, and has led, to the loss of the prophet's primary message. We can be fairly certain that Micah would be seriously disappointed if he were remembered only because he spoke of a ruler coming from Bethlehem. If such wagers could ever be collected, it would be a safe one that Micah would rather be remembered as the champion of the poor and of the downtrodden and as the fearless denouncer of social injustice. He and Amos saw eye to prophetic eye.

5.

ISAIAH

ISAIAH'S CALL TO PROPHECY

ONE of the characteristics of the literature of ancient Israel is that it was constantly being adapted to the changing historical scene. This could be done in many different ways. A later writer could, for example, add new laws to the older collections, or fill out a prophetic oracle with an application to the contemporary situation. Again, an older passage could be edited to bring it up to date, or whole new chapters could be added to the primitive core.

This may strike us as strange. This is because of the modern concept of authorship which is considered so individual an effort that it is securely protected by copyrights of all kinds. Before the decided multiplication of books in the early Christian era authorship, especially in the area of religious literature, was a community project to a great extent. Unabashed and free use was made of the heritage of the past to compose a new work which was in turn considered common property. The community, responsible for the creation and development of the literature, was also responsible for its proper preservation, thus protecting it to an extent from the unauthorized additions or adaptations of the fringe members of society. Israel's religious literature, which for practical purposes is all that has survived, thus became so intimate a part of her whole life that it was constantly being brought up to date. We can compare it to modern prayer books which are constantly being revised; very seldom do we know who the original author was. In other words, Israel practiced a constant literary *aggiornamento*. That is why her literature never lost its dynamic character throughout her long and varied history; her literature always said something appropriate to the times.

The prophetic literature was no exception. It, too, was kept alive. Sometimes, therefore, it is difficult to know just what belongs to the historical prophet and what was added later. And yet it is important to know as best we can so that we can evaluate each prophet more accurately by his authentic writings. In the case of Isaiah quite a bit of editorial work took place. Although our present book contains some 66 chapters, it is commonly agreed that chapters 40 to 66 were added much later, 150 years or more after Isaiah himself. We will consider these chapters later. Even chapter 1 to 39 are not all from Isaiah himself. In our study of the prophet, therefore, we will be careful to use only what is certainly authentic.

When we studied Micah we saw something of the political and economic situation in Judah. The reign of King Uzziah had been a long one (783–742 B.C.) and marked by prosperity and peace. As in Israel, the nation was fat with success. Micah, as we saw, was not impressed by the success. There was another one, destined to become far greater than Micah, who likewise was unimpressed. His name was Isaiah.

Isaiah apparently belonged to an important family, one that had shared, no doubt, in the general prosperity. But this young aristocrat had somehow kept his personal integrity; he wanted nothing of tainted success. Possibly he had read the burning oracles of Amos and even of Micah, and he would at least have heard of Hosea and his message. The words of these men of God remained with him and helped to shape his own religious convictions which were soon to burst forth in an inspired torrent that would really make Jerusalem and all of Judah know that a prophet was in their midst.

What determined Isaiah on his mission was a vision that he had of the Lord, Yahweh. It was a most impressive one. It not only proved a clear call to the prophetic office but also had much to do with the manner in which he fulfilled that office. The vision is recorded in chapter 6 of the book. It occurred, we are told there, in the year that Uzziah died, 742 B.C. The young man was likely attending a liturgical function in the temple of Jerusalem. The singing of the choir, the swirling of the incense smoke, the formal gestures of the priests all raised the youth's mind and heart to the contemplation of the majesty of God. Suddenly, he saw God Himself in vision, enthroned in heaven! Seraphim (some kind of angelic beings) hovered about the throne crying out, "Holy, holy, holy is the Lord of hosts!"

The Hebrew word for "holy" comes from a root word meaning to "cut off." One is holy, then, when one is cut off, or separated from that which is profane or unclean. God is thrice holy (the Hebrews had no superlative form), which is to say that He is the most transcendent of all beings. There is none like Him; nothing created can in any way be compared to Him. Notice the reaction of Isaiah. So impressed is he by what he sees and, above all, by the surpassing holiness of Yahweh that he is only aware of his own creaturehood. What part can he have with the majestic God? "For I am a man of unclean lips, living among a people of unclean lips; yet my eyes have seen the King, the Lord of hosts!" We are reminded of the reaction of Peter to the

84

manifestation of Jesus's power at the extraordinary catch of fish: "Depart from me, for I am a sinful man, O Lord!" (Lk 5:8). This is the necessary reaction of creature-man when God reveals to him His glory.

But the vision is not yet complete. If this had been all, it is unlikely that Isaiah would have been emboldened to go out and preach the word of this God. We read, therefore, that one of the seraphim touched the young man's lips with a burning coal, indicating the cleansing of his sins and the divine approval of his mission. Then when the Lord, still in vision, asks who will go and preach His message, the young Isaiah cries out unhesitatingly, "Here I am; send me!" This is the response, unaffected and direct, of one who recognizes a true vocation and accepts it. Here is a man not afraid to become involved.

The message he must preach, as he shortly learns, is not one of life and hope, but one of doom. His words will only have the effect of hardening the hearts of his listeners until final destruction overcomes them. What a terrifying apostolate this was, to know in advance that your message would not be heard and yet to preach it as though it must be heard; to know that your threats of doom, intended to move to repentance, would actually be fulfilled because there was none that repented. Not many could have the courage or the zeal, and especially the faith to accept such a mission. We can readily imagine that the one thing that kept Isaiah strong in faith was the memory of this vision. That overpowering scene, centered on the majestic God, was to color many of his oracles. We can understand now how he could be so horrified by the rebellion of God's people, for he had seen the God against whom they were rebelling.

Isaiah is one of the really great figures of the whole Old Testament. This is true, not so much because of the effect he had on his own contemporaries, since most of them refused to listen to him, but because of the innate power and beauty of his oracles. Fortunately, his disciples recognized this power and beauty and preserved his words. And later generations of Israel gave their witness to his greatness by adding other oracles, composed in the spirit of the prophet, to the original collection.

Outside of his prophecies we know almost nothing about Isaiah. From these prophecies we can gather that his ministry coincided with the reigns of Jotham (742–735), Ahaz (735–715) and Hezekiah (715–687). We learn, too, that he was married and had at least two sons whose symbolic names summarized his own inspired message. Isaiah reacted to critical times without compromise. The last half of the eighth century b.c. was witnessing a rapid increase in Assyrian power and domination. All the smaller nations bordering on the Mediterranean were fearful of this giant. Even the king of Judah was prepared for abject submission. Only Isaiah stood firm, strong in his faith in the power of God, the Lord of hosts.

ISAIAH AND RELIGION IN JUDAH

It is much more difficult to sum up the work of Isaiah than that of Amos or Hosea. While the latter two apparently broke in upon society to bring divine judgment upon it for a comparatively brief span of time, Isaiah exercised his prophetic office throughout his lifetime. His earliest oracles were probably delivered during the reign of Jotham (742–735); and he was extremely active during the reigns of both Ahaz (735–715) and Hezekiah (715–687). We will study the prophet in the light of various aspects of his ministry but against the historical back-ground that was dominated by these three kings. It is important therefore to review in a summary fashion this background if we would understand Isaiah.

Jotham's reign was really a continuation of the long reign of Uzziah (783–742). The period was one of peace and prosperity which had engendered a false sense of security in the people, and a conviction that the Lord fully approved all their activities. They felt they must be living good, God-fearing lives. From the very beginning of his new apostolate Isaiah told them quite bluntly that they were absolutely wrong, and warned that peril would overtake them if they did not reform. This message of denunci-ation and of threat of punishment characterized his ministry during the reign of Jotham.

In the reign of Ahaz it required no prophet to see the peril threatening Judah. Assyria was developing an army that was clearly intended for more than national defense. All the smaller nations to the west of Assyria along the Mediterranean coast busied themselves with forming what, in today's language, could be called EMTO, the Eastern Mediterranean Treaty Organization. The northern kingdom of Israel and Damascus, the foremost city-state of Syria, seemed to be the principal instigators. The problem facing Judah in the person of Ahaz, its king, was whether to join this alliance against the threat from the east or to remain neutral. Isaiah urged a policy of no foreign alliances of any kind.

Ahaz did remain neutral, at least for a time. But his reasons were not those of Isaiah who had encouraged complete trust in God. The king feared the wrath of Assyria if he joined the anti-Assyrian plot. The poverty of his faith was manifested somewhat later when the two kingdoms of Israel and Damascus declared war on their southern neighbor in order to force him into the alliance. Judah's king then made the move that Assyria was probably hoping for all along; he cravenly besought its king, Tiglath-pileser III, for help. Eagerly, Assyria pitched in. In 734 b.c. Israel was invaded and ravaged, saved from complete destruction only by the succession of a new king who was more docile to the foreign master. A bit later, Damascus met a similar fate.

The guise of neutrality shattered, Ahaz had now to make public witness of his submission to Assyria, paying tribute and even honoring its pagan gods. It was this lack of faith in God that made Isaiah so contemptuous of the king and of all those who fled immediately to material means in time of need. It was this lack of faith, he was convinced, that led to all the disasters that overtook God's people. Later on in the reign of Ahaz he could have pointed to the fate of the northern kingdom which, in the year 721 b.c., was completely overwhelmed by the Assyrians. Israel, as a political entity, ceased to exist; Isaiah would have interpreted this as the wages of infidelity.

The third period of the prophet's activity was that of King Hezekiah who inherited from his father, Ahaz, the situation of vassalage to Assyria. But he was a much more religious man than his father and frequently consulted the prophet, Isaiah. He did not, however, invariably follow the seer's advice. On one occasion he succumbed to the temptation to join in an alliance against Assyria. As Isaiah had predicted, the inevitable happened. Judah was invaded in 701 b.c. and much of the territory was devastated. But, while despair filled the hearts of all, Isaiah predicted that Jerusalem would not fall. In some mysterious way the prediction was verified. Sennacherib, the Assyrian conqueror, left without taking the capital city, but he exacted a heavy tribute on Hezekiah. The tribute was a sign of his vassalage, the political situation that continued throughout the last years of the prophet.

The first chapter of *Isaiah* should be read against this complex background. It contains a collection of his oracles made at different times but magnificently summarizing his inspired message. Note the strong figures he uses to chastize the people. They are worse than oxen or asses who at least can recognize where they sleep and who is their master. Note especially how, with biting satire, he denounces their formalistic worship: a people going through the motions of worship but whose hearts are far from God. How often in history could Isaiah have repeated this! How appropriate even in our own day!

Hear, O heavens, and listen, O earth, for the Lord speaks; sons have I raised and reared, but they have disowned me! An ox knows its owner, and an ass, its master's manger; but Israel does not know, my people has not understood. Ah! sinful nation, people laden with wickedness, evil race, corrupt children! They have forsaken the Lord, spurned the Holy One of Israel, apostatized. . . . What care I for the number of your sacrifices? says the Lord. I have had enough of whole-burnt rams and fat of fatlings; in the blood of calves, lambs and goats I find no pleasure. When you come in to visit me, who asks these things of you? Trample my courts no more! Bring no more worthless offerings; your incense is loathsome to me. New moon and sabbath, calling of assemblies, octaves with wickedness: these I cannot bear. . . . When you spread out your hands, I close my eyes to you; though you pray the more, I will not listen. Your hands are full of blood! Wash yourselves clean! Put away your misdeeds from before my eyes; cease doing evil; learn to do good. Make justice your aim; redress the wronged, hear the orphan's plea, defend the widow (vv. 2–4. 11–13. 15–17).

One of the first oracles of Isaiah is the famous "Vineyard Song" in chapter 5. It describes the tender love that a man has for his vineyard, a love strengthened by much sacrifice for it. But that love is not repaid and now he must destroy his work. All of this Isaiah's listeners could understand with sympathy. But then he turns upon his complacent audience and identifies *them* as the vineyard of the Lord (v. 7)! Isaiah has set the tone for his ministry:

Let me now sing of my friend, my friend's song concerning his vineyard. My friend had a vineyard on a fertile hillside; he spaded it, cleared it of stones, and planted the choicest vines; within it he built a watchtower, and hewed out a wine press. Then he looked for the crop of grapes, but what it yielded was wild grapes. . . . The vineyard of the Lord of hosts is the house of Israel, and the men of Juda are his cherished plant; he looked for judgment, but see, bloodshed! for justice, but hark, the outcry! (vv. 1–2. 7).

Another powerful passage from this early period is his satirical description of the women of Jerusalem (3:16—4:1) to which we referred when considering Amos. Here in the glaring light of God's reality are exposed all the petty vanities, coquetries, mannerisms and extravagances of dress, ornamentation and make-up of the women of every age. What woman can read this passage and not see at least a little of herself described in its lines?

The Lord said: Because the daughters of Sion are haughty, and walk with necks outstretched ogling and mincing as they go, their anklets tinkling with every step, the Lord shall cover the scalps of Sion's daughters with scabs, and the Lord shall bare their heads. On that day the Lord will do away with the finery of the anklets, sunbursts, and crescents; the pendants, bracelets, and veils; the headdresses, bangles, cinctures, perfume boxes, and amulets; the signet rings, and the nose rings; the court dresses, wraps, cloaks, and purses; the mirrors, linen tunics, turbans, and shawls (3:16–23).

The satire of this passage is quite in line with what had just preceded, where the prophet had castigated the rulers of Judah.

So rapacious and godless are they that a society built on them cannot stand. And its collapse will be so total that in the new situation anyone who has clothes on his back will be considered affluent enough to take over the rule (3:6). It is possible that Isaiah, knowing what kind of man Ahaz was, predicted this collapse towards the beginning of the new king's reign. If so, Ahaz knew from the outset how he stood in Isaiah's eyes. Isaiah, as we already mentioned, judged everything in the light of his inaugural vision. He served a God before whom pettiness and hypocrisy were revealed for what they really were. Isaiah's religion asked of a man that he repent of his sins and stand firm in God. Religion as it was practiced in Judah was not up to this standard. And it revealed its weaknesses in the various crises that overtook the land.

The crisis of the war with Israel and Damascus we will consider in the next section because of its connection with the messianic oracle. Here we can take a look at the crisis brought on by Sennacherib's invasion of Judah in 701 B.C., described above. Several passages in our book date from that period, although they are now scattered in different chapters. One very powerful oracle is found in 10:5-34. The first long section, verses 5-27, is directed against Assyria itself. Composed at a time when that nation had asserted its power throughout the Near East and when Judah herself lay helpless before the world power, this oracle, wrung from a boundless faith in God, declares that this seemingly invincible force is but a pawn in the hand of the Almighty. God is using Assyria as a rod of anger against His sinning people:

Woe to Assyria! My rod in anger, my staff in wrath. Against an impious nation I send him, and against a people under my wrath I order him to seize plunder, carry off loot, and tread them down like the mud of the streets (10:5–6).

But Assyria, in her pagan pride, does not accept this explanation. "By my own power I have done it, and by my wisdom, for I am shrewd," she says (vv. 13–14). Little does Assyria know that she is but an axe in the hand of God who hews with it, and no axe can rebel against its user (vv. 15–16). Isaiah goes on, then, to show the ultimate purpose of all this history: the return of at least a remnant of His people to Him:

On that day the remnant of Israel, the survivors of the house of Jacob, will no more lean upon him who struck them; but they will lean upon the Lord, the Holy One of Israel, in truth. A remnant will return, the remnant of Jacob, to the mighty God. For though your people, O Israel, were like the sand of the sea, only a remnant of them will return; their destruction is decreed as overwhelming justice demands (10:20–22).

The mention of the remnant evokes an important theological concept of the Old Testament to which Isaiah made his contribution. In its special technical sense it refers to that part of Israel which will escape God's judgment of destruction and which will thus be the necessary instrument of continuing salvation. St. Paul was later to quote from our passage here, and sees it fulfilled in the early Jewish converts to Christianity (Rom 9:27).

The same crisis is reflected in 29:1–16. Here the emphasis is on the stupidity and spiritual blindness of the people of Judah:

Be irresolute, stupefied; blind yourselves and stay blind! Be drunk, but not from wine, stagger, but not from strong drink! For the Lord has poured out on you a spirit of deep sleep. He has shut your eyes [the prophets] and covered your heads [the seers] (vv. 9–10).

This is the cause of all the evil that comes upon them (vv. 1–8). The meaning of the strange statement in verse 10 is that, when man rebels against God, God punishes him with the gradual loss of his moral sense. This is happening to God's people.

A final message from the same general period is found in 30:8–17. Before the smugness of a people who do not want to hear the prophet's warnings, Isaiah writes down on a tablet his predictions of woe. Then a future generation will know at least that faith has seen more clearly than national pride, that trust in God was a greater security than much arms or many allies:

> Now come, write it on a tablet they can keep, inscribe it in a record; that it may be in future days an eternal witness: This is a rebellious people, deceitful children, children who refuse to obey the law of the Lord. . . . Therefore, thus says the Holy One of Israel: Because you reject this word, and put your trust in what is crooked and devious, and depend on it, this guilt of yours shall be like a descending rift bulging out in a high wall whose crash comes suddenly, in an instant (30:8–9. 12–13).

If we were to sum up the religion of Isaiah in one word, that word would be "faith." And by faith we mean a personal commitment to the living God by reason of which he could see with the eyes of God. It was this faith of the prophet that contrasted with the faith of Judah which was expressed in the false security of foreign alliances and meaningless attention to the external forms of worship. Despite the seeming odds against it, Isaiah's faith would win out.

ISAIAH AND THE MESSIANIC PRINCE

In our study of Isaiah we take up the question of messianism which we consider briefly in our introductory chapter, as well as in *Micah*. It will come up again in later prophets. It is found in several of the *Psalms*. And it is basic for understanding the coming of Jesus in a Jewish world. But before we study messianism in *Isaiah,* let us quickly review its roots in Israel's history.

Through her sacred history and the part played by God in making that history possible, Israel learned to look forward to a great day. It would be a day when the reason why God saved Israel would find its adequate explanation. It would be a great "saving" day that would climax all of salvation history. Israel gradually realized that this day would be marked by another special intervention of God's, as in the exodus from Egypt. Gradually, too, she realized that a special representative of God's would come to bring about this salvation. And, since David had been promised an everlasting throne, this special representative was first pictured as a "son of David," a royal descendant of Israel's greatest king. There would be other ways in which this special representative would be described, as we shall see, but the first descriptions portrayed him as a Davidic prince. And since the kings of Israel were all anointed, it is natural that this future king would be called "*the* anointed one." In Hebrew this is *messiah,* in Greek *christos*. And that is why Jesus is called the messiah, or, according to the Greek, the Christ.

Coming back to *Isaiah* now, the first passage that interests us is in chapter 7. We saw the background of this in the preceding section. The kings of Damascus and Israel are besieging Judah to force its king, Ahaz, to join the anti-Assyrian alliance. Isaiah meets the king, at the Lord's command, and tells him not to fear these invaders from the north (Is 7:1-8). He insists that Ahaz puts his trust in God alone. In fact, Isaiah tells him that God will perform a sign for him, anything he wishes, if he will only trust wholly in the Lord. But Ahaz is afraid; God just might perform such a sign! Then he would be bound to listen to the prophet's advice. This he does not want to do; he rejects the offer (7:10–12).

God, however, will give him a sign whether he likes it or not. Through His prophet He says that "the virgin shall be with child, and bear a son, and shall name him Emmanuel. He shall be living on curds and honey by the time he learns to reject the bad and choose the good. For before the child learns to reject the bad and choose the good, the land of those two kings whom you dread shall be deserted" (7:14–15).

As Christians we learn from Matthew's Gospel that this prophecy was perfectly fulfilled in the birth of Jesus Christ, some seven hundred years after Isaiah's day (see Matt 1:22–23). Mary is the virgin and Jesus is "Emmanuel," that is, "God with us." But it must be remembered that this interpretation was given in the light of a developing revelation which Isaiah did not completely share. Moreover, if we are correct in saying that the prophets were men involved in their own times, we can suspect that they were not giving off oracles that had relevance only for a period of history some seven hundred years later. We would suppose, therefore, that Isaiah thought his words had some contemporary relevance, that they meant something to the people of his own day. And when we read the words in their context, as quoted above, we realize that Isaiah was giving a sign that he thought would be realized, at least in some way, *in his own lifetime*. He says that the child, whose birth he predicts, would still be an infant when the lands of the two invading kings would be devastated.

In what way, then, would the prophecy of mother and child have been realized in the history of the southern kingdom? The problem is most complex and has been the object of countless scholarly books and monographs. The more commonly accepted explanation can be summarized in this way. First of all, we need not suppose that the prophet is speaking of a miraculous virgin birth such as was verified in the case of Jesus and Mary. While the Hebrew word that is used does suggest virginity (it refers more properly to an unmarried girl who is ready for marriage), this would mean that she was a virgin at the time the prophet spoke. Likely she was a young maid recently introduced into the king's harem in whom the people and the king now placed their hopes for a royal son and the continuation of the dynasty. That son, as Isaiah foresaw, was born; he was the young prince, Hezekiah. And before Hezekiah reached the use of reason, Assyria had come in power against Israel and Damascus, as we have already seen. Thus were the two lands "deserted" and Isaiah's sign fulfilled.

This, however, does not exhaust the meaning of the words. If this is God's word, as we believe, then it is surely patient of a developing interpretation in the light of developing salvation history. And it is precisely because of this divine potential latent in the oracle that the later evangelist could say with such assurance that the birth of Jesus had *fulfilled* the prophecy of Isaiah, that the event had brought out for the man of faith the fullness of meaning of an ancient prophecy.

A more difficult question concerns Isaiah's own understanding of the oracle. That he saw it as applied to Hezekiah, as explained above, seems certain. But did he see more than this? Did he perhaps see Hezekiah as a type, or foreshadowing, of the great messianic prince to come on the "day of the Lord"? Of course, he did not think of Jesus and Mary as we know them. But Isaiah was a man of tremendous faith in Yahweh. This is evident in the offer he made to Ahaz; he had no doubt that God could do whatever Ahaz asked. Given such a faith and given the prophet's convictions about the meaning and destiny of history, it is difficult to imagine that he thought God's purpose was exhausted in the events of his own day. Men with the faith of Isaiah think bigger thoughts than that.

This is somewhat confirmed by the passage in 8:23–9:6. Here we read, first, of the deep gloom that settled on the land of the northern kingdom. This was a result of the Assyrian invasion which we have already considered. But gloom gives way to joy, darkness to light, as there is announced the birth (or the enthronement) of a new prince in David's house:

The people who walked in darkness have seen a great light; upon those who dwelt in the land of gloom a light has shone. . . . For a child is born to us, a son is given us; upon his shoulder dominion rests (9:1. 5).

Again, we can suppose that the prophet is thinking, first of all, of the accession of Hezekiah to the throne. That day was celebrated with much ceremony in Israel. It was a kind of second birthday when the newly anointed king took on a new name and a new life. Great things would be predicted of him by the court poets. But Isaiah was no court poet fashioning flowery, flattering verses for the king. When he describes this king and Israel's hopes for him, he is moved to express his own hopes, born of a deep faith in God, for the ideal leader who would one day come just as surely as Hezekiah had come. He felt no hesitation, therefore, in calling him "Wonder-Counselor, God-Hero, Father-Forever, Prince of Peace." These descriptive names were more than just part of the royal court style; for Isaiah they expressed perfectly what the great God could achieve and would achieve one day.

Still another description is given in 11:1-9. It fills in our picture. It describes a shoot that would come from the "stump of Jesse," that is, the house of David, and the gifts of the spirit of God that would be his: "a spirit of wisdom and of understanding, a spirit of counsel and of strength, a spirit of knowledge and of fear of the Lord . . . " They are gifts of the mind and heart that would enable him to judge wisely and rule well.

In the latter part of the oracle (vv. 6-9) we read about the idyllic conditions that will prevail then, about the peace and harmony that will characterize the period: "Then the wolf shall be a guest of the lamb, and the leopard shall lie down with the kid; the calf and the young lion shall browse together, with a child to guide them." The description is not to be taken literally. Writers of ancient times often described the rule of the perfect king in these figures. But our main interest is in the king. Is the "shoot" from "Jesse's stump" to be identified with the young Hezekiah whose reign anticipates, even if but dimly, the glorious reign of the future Messiah?

This is a possible explanation. On the other hand, it is also possible to see a progression in Isaiah's thought throughout these various descriptions. The "Emmanuel" of 7:14 is Ahaz' son, soon to be born. But the brief reference would have already given the prophet the occasion to foresee, dimly, another Emmanuel in the future. The latter figure takes on a clearer perspective in 8:23-9:6 when Hezekiah's coronation day gives him the occasion to express his great hopes for the future. Finally, in 11:1-9 we find the climactic expression of Isaiah's faith in the future redeemer.

Such a progression in the prophet's thought is quite under-standable in the light of the developing situation. In the latter part of his ministry Isaiah would have recalled the weak and vacillating kings of the past; these, it is not necessary to insist, were hardly the divine representatives to fulfill glorious hopes. Thus a greater concentration on the day of the Lord with its special messianic representative would have been encouraged. He could describe this prince now, not as an expression of vague hope, but as a certainty guaranteed by the steadfast will of Yahweh to save His people. But whatever the precise meanings intended by Isaiah in these several oracles, his contribution to the messianic hope, occasioned by the royal house of David of his day, would add to his luster as one of the great prophets of the Old Testament.

ISAIAH AND THE NATIONS

One of the difficulties faced by Christians when they read the Old Testament is the attitude of the sacred authors to the pagan nations. We can understand that they would not pray for their success in war, for the expansion of their empires, or even for their political well-being. But the attitude is not simply a nega-tive one; it is a very positive one that finds expression in some of the most virulent language in ancient literature. The nations, or *goyim,* are to be conquered and annihilated, and God was asked to bring this about.

The origins of this attitude can be traced back to the days before Israel possessed the land. Coming up from slavery in Egypt she was aware that the land of Canaan, the land of the patriarchs, was not lying there unoccupied, waiting for the coming of God's people. In fact, she had a bitter experience of what she had to face when an invasion attempt was made from the south shortly after the events at Mount Sinai. We read that "the Amalecites and Chanaanites who dwelt in that hill country came down and defeated them . . . " (Num 14:45).

Whatever might have been said about the *promised* land, therefore, Israel knew that it was not going to be handed to her by God on a silver platter. And yet she did expect the Lord to assist her in obtaining it. She would have to fight for the land, but she was fully confident that the Lord would be the invisible captain of the fighting forces. A very ancient song, sung by Israel as she carried the Ark of the Covenant, the symbol of God's presence, out into battle, went like this: "Arise, O Lord, that your enemies may be scattered, and those who hate you may flee before you" (Num 10:35).

This primitive war chant gives us a good insight into the attitude towards the nations that was developed by Israel. Her enemies, basically, are God's enemies. If they hate Israel, it must be that they hate her God who made them His people. Since He had not made these others His people, it must be that He has rejected them. Israel, then, must also reject them. This rejection was all the more imperative because they worshipped false gods. While these gods were no threat to Yahweh, impotent as they were in the face of His supreme power, still they were a danger to God's people. Israel could be led to forget her oath of loyalty to the one God and to render "wanton worship to their gods and sacrifice to them" (Ex 34:15). It was because of this danger that we read that ". . . when the Lord, your God, delivers them (the enemies) up to you and you defeat them, you shall doom them. . . . Tear down their altars, smash their sacred pillars, chop

100

down their sacred poles, and destroy their idols by fire. For you are a people sacred to the Lord, your God . . . " (Deut 7:2.5–6).

To the extent that this attitude was based on the religious convictions of one true God and of His choice of Israel, it was perfectly justified. It could and did lead to a false exclusiveness at times: the pagans could not be the object of God's saving power. It could occasion extreme measures in time of war, such as the wiping out of all the inhabitants of a city in holy zeal (see Jos 6:21). It could express itself in cursing Psalms that shock the Christian reader. But all of this God permitted in order that the basic truth of the attitude might live on. There *was* but one God and Israel *was* His chosen people. Once these truths, together with all they rightly implied, were deeply rooted in Israel's soul (and the prophets show us that it took a long time), then would God show them the true role of the gentiles in the plan of salvation. But we would have to wait until the New Testament period for the fullness of that revelation.

In Isaiah's time they were still far from understanding all that God's moral will implied. They had linked their national safety and independence with the power of their God. To an extent, Yahweh was willing to respect this criterion. If they observed the covenant in all its dimensions, if they put their trust solely in Yahweh, if above all they worshipped Him, not alone with external feasts and many prayers, but deep within their hearts, then He would save them and prove Himself their God. The step from this to the conviction that Israel's enemies would learn what it was to be enemies of the one God's chosen people was an easy one.

The nobler souls in Israel could foresee the day when the

pagan nations would learn of the God of Israel and would come to the mount of Jerusalem to be instructed in the Law. Isaiah was one of these (see Is 2:2–4). But the idea was a hard one for Israel to accept; it would take a long time to be developed. Meanwhile, the pagan nations would play out their role as the enemies of God and of His people.

Oracles against the pagan nations were probably a recognized and expected part of the prophetic ministry. For a people that loved concrete images and bold contrasts, an ideal way to bring home God's choice of them was to begin with a statement of His rejection of others. We saw that Amos began his prophecy with a series of "woes" against the neighbors of Israel. Ordinarily, the series would be climaxed by a jubilant prediction of salvation for Israel, a prediction made all the more joyous by the contrasting "woe" of the nations. But Amos turned the tables on Israel by including her in the series of "woes." Israel, he says in effect, is no better than a pagan nation in God's sight. And that, for Israel, was the most bitter judgment of all.

We cannot appreciate the effectiveness of Amos' stratagem, of course, unless we understand this attitude about the *goyim*. Then, too, will we better understand why almost all the prophets have their oracles to deliver against the foreign nations. In *Isaiah* they are all conveniently collected in chapters 13 to 23. Not all of these were delivered by the historical Isaiah. Chapter 13, for example, and the first 23 verses of chapter 14 have to do with the fall of Babylon. But Babylon was no threat to Judah in Isaiah's day. She was subject to Assyria, which was the great power of the time. Also it refers to the Medes (13:17) who, along with the Persians, did bring an end to Babylon, but some 150 years later. For some reason, perhaps because of the power of the language, the oracle was added to the collection of Isaiah.

An especially powerful part of this oracle is the so-called taunt song in 14:4b–21. It ranks as one of the more dramatic pieces of the Old Testament and should be read aloud. It is a taunt flung at a proud city that had boasted mightily of its deeds, but that was now doomed to destruction. It would be applied to any tyrant or any nation that reckons without God.

The short section that follows, an oracle against Assyria, comes from Isaiah. It is rather strange that this is the only prophecy we have by the prophet against the great Assyrian nation. If he uttered oracles against the other nations he would surely have pronounced them against the one great enemy of his day. But all we have are these few verses. This leads some scholars to think that the taunt song against Babylon, which we just saw, was originally composed as an oracle against Assyria and later changed. This is in accord with the constant process of adaptation that Israel's literature underwent.

Chapters 15 and 16 contain an oracle against Moab. Really it is a dirge that describes some catastrophe that has overwhelmed the country. Scholars are uncertain as to what event is being depicted here, and so are not sure of the date or the author. At any rate, the picture that is painted is one of rare beauty. The refugees struggling along with their few remaining possessions on their back present a pitiful sight. For Israel it was the picture of every man who does not know the true God. Moab was among these; her fate is not unexpected.

Chapter 17 contains a collection of various oracles. Only the first three verses refer to Damascus, that great city to the north of Israel that had brought so much trouble on God's people in years gone by. Her fate will be that of all of God's enemies. The last three verses no doubt were originally spoken of Assyria who would come with great hordes against the chosen people:

Ah! the roaring of many peoples that roar like the roar of the seas!
The surging of nations that surge like the surging of mighty waves!
(17:12).

But they, too, before God are "like chaff on the mountain, like
tumbleweed in a storm" (v. 13). The verses in between seemingly
apply to the northern kingdom, whose fall in 721 B.C. occurred
during Isaiah's ministry. Note the expression "on that day," one
first used by Amos and identified by him as a day of doom for
the faithless people. Isaiah takes up the theme and spells it out
more clearly.

Chapters 18–20 bring us into the midst of international politics. With Assyria's growth in power and gradual expansion to
the west, the other powers like Ethiopia and Egypt begin plot-
ting. They want to sow dissension among Assyria's satellites. But,
as Isaiah sees it, they are only puppets acting out a game. If they
do not take Yahweh into account, they act in vain.

The remaining oracles in this collection, except for chapter 22,
are similarly concerned with the pagan nations. As with the
others there is really only one theme here. No matter how great
the power, or how ancient the city, or how prosperous the
princes, these is only one master of their destiny. That is Yahweh, and He is the God of Israel. "The Lord of hosts has planned
it, to disgrace all pride of majesty, to degrade all the earth's hon-
ored men. . . . His hand he stretches out over the sea, he shakes
kingdoms; the Lord has ordered the destruction of Chanaan's
strongholds" (23:9.11).

6.

JEREMIAH

JEREMIAH'S INAUGURAL VISION

WE come now to the second of the so-called major prophets, Jeremiah, son of Hilkiah, of a priestly family in Anathoth, in the land of Benjamin (Jer 1:1). Like Isaiah, Jeremiah prophesied over a long period of time. Like him, too, he left behind a number of oracles that were gradually collected to form a book of considerable length; there are 52 chapters in *Jeremiah*. Finally, as with Isaiah, the prophecies of Jeremiah were edited and added to in the course of time.

Despite these similarities, there are marked differences between the two, and the collections of their prophecies. There is no "Second Jeremiah" to correspond to Second Isaiah; the editorial and other additions to the book are neither extensive nor characteristic enough to be the work of any one editor or author. Also, in *Jeremiah* we find a long section, chapters 26–45, that is narrative in form and which is mostly the account, by Baruch, Jeremiah's secretary, of the prophet's various adventures. Interspersed in the account are several oracles by the prophet concerning Israel and Judah.

As we might expect, *Jeremiah*, too, has a collection of oracles against the nations (chs. 46–51). As in Isaiah, these have been edited by later authors. In fact, this part has probably been added to more than any other section of the book. All in all, however, more has been preserved of the prophet Jeremiah than of Isaiah. There is no doubt that Baruch, Jeremiah's secretary, is chiefly responsible for this (see ch. 36).

One more important difference between Isaiah and Jeremiah is the historical background. Isaiah was about God's business during the last part of the eighth century and the first part of the seventh. He witnessed the fall of the northern kingdom in 721 B.C., and he dealt with kings of such differing characters as Ahaz and Hezekiah. Jeremiah, on the other hand, spoke God's word in the latter part of the seventh and first part of the sixth century. He witnessed the fall of his own kingdom, Judah, in 587 B.C., while dealing with kings like Josiah and Zedekiah.

A brief review of this background is essential for understanding the prophet's message. When he first began his public ministry, Josiah was reigning as king of Judah. The latter had come to the throne in 640 B.C. after the religiously disastrous reigns of Manasseh (687–642) and Amon (642–640). He embarked upon a serious program of reform which is described in some detail in *2 Kings* 22–23. Had Josiah lived longer than he did and in more peaceful circumstances, the reform might have been more successful than it was. But other events were brewing which would change the course of history.

Ever since the middle of the preceding century, Assyria had been the great world power whom all nations feared. Judah, among many others, had long been her vassal. Another vassal, Babylon, to the south of Assyria, had made several moves towards regaining independence but none had succeeded. But Babylon continued to grow in power and, in the latter half of the seventh century, became a real threat to Assyria. The end came swiftly when Nabopolassar took control of Babylon's army. In 612 B.C.

Nineveh, Assyria's capital, fell, and a few years later the last Assyrian stronghold was captured. Babylon was now mistress of the world.

In the meantime, Egypt, fearing the rise of a new and unknown power, had sent an army through Palestine to northern Mesopotamia to help Assyria in her desperate stand. Josiah, Judah's king, rejoicing over what was happening to the ancient enemies of God's people and not wanting anything to hinder their downfall, took an army against the Egyptians to stop them from going to Assyria's aid. In the battle Josiah died, an unnecessary victim for a cause that had already been decided. It was 609 B.C.

Josiah was succeeded by Jehoahaz. But the Egyptians, now temporarily in control, deposed him and placed Jehoiakim instead on the throne. Jehoiakim reigned from 609 to 598. By this time Nabopolassar had been succeeded in Babylon by his son, Nebuchadnezzar, who decided to consolidate the western part of his empire. In 604 B.C. he advanced with an army and took Jerusalem without a struggle. Judah, under Jehoiakim, was vassal now to Babylon as she was once to Assyria. About 598 B.C. Jehoiakim attempted to rebel against Babylon. Again Nebuchadnezzar came in power. After a siege of several months, Jerusalem fell. Many of the people, including much of the nobility, were deported to Babylon, and a heavy tribute was exacted. During the siege, Jehoiakim had died and was succeeded by his son, Jehoiachin. This young king was among those deported to Babylon; he remained there as a prisoner for some 37 years. On Judah's throne Nebuchadnezzar now placed Jehoiachin's uncle, Mattaniah, whose name he changed to Zedekiah. He was to be Judah's last king.

For a time, Zedekiah followed Jeremiah's advice and refrained from attempts at independence. Finally, urged on by his anti-Babylonian court, he rebelled. Once again, the reaction was swift. Nebuchadnezzar came, surrounded the city of Jerusalem and, after a long siege, breached its walls. Zedekiah was taken prisoner, a large number of people deported, the temple destroyed and the city looted. Judah was no more.

Jeremiah lived through all of this, his advice disregarded and even misinterpreted and his own person subjected to grave indignities. At the end he was given his choice by Babylon of remaining behind with the poor of the razed city or of being taken to Babylon. He chose the former. A few years later, after a senseless attack by some rebel elements against the governor placed by Nebuchadnezzar over the territory, Jeremiah was forced by these rebels to accompany them in flight to Egypt. There he continued to preach until his death.

It is clear from this brief summary that Jeremiah lived through one of the most critical periods of Israel's long history. In fact, crisis followed crisis and our prophet was intimately involved in most of them. We wonder, then, what kind of man this was whom God had chosen to preside over such a decisive moment of His people's history. If we had been the lords of destiny, it is more than likely that our choice would have fallen on a strong-minded man, an extrovert in the finest sense of the word, on one who could brave the "slings and arrows of outrageous fortune" with quiet dignity and resignation. But God's ways, we learn so frequently in the Scriptures, are not man's ways. So we need to ask whom the true Lord of all destinies did choose for this critical task. One of the clearest indications is provided in the opening chapter of his book, the description of his vocation.

Recall for a moment, for reasons of contrast, the vision accorded Isaiah (Is 6:1–13). We noted how the aristocratic youth at first was overwhelmed by the majesty of the Lord. But purified by the burning coal, he responded immediately and eagerly to God's plea for a spokesman (6:8). Isaiah's "Here I am; send me!" is the answer of an outspoken, self-assured young man with few inhibitions. In the call of Jeremiah we find two principal points of contrast. The first is in the Lord's manner of dealing with His future spokesman. Here we have no sweeping vision of cosmic proportions, with seraphim and incense smoke, royal throne and shattering cry of angels. Rather, here there is only the intimate dialogue between two who are already friends (Jer 1:4–8). Here there is no burning coal held by angelic hand to cleanse the prophet's lips. Rather, here the Lord Himself places His hand gently on His spokesman's mouth (Jer 1:9):

The word of the Lord came to me thus: Before I formed you in the womb I knew you, before you were born I dedicated you, a prophet to the nations I appointed you. "Ah, Lord God!" I said, "I know not how to speak; I am too young." But the Lord answered me, Say not, "I am too young." To whomever I send you, you shall go; whatever I command you, you shall speak. Have no fear before them, because I am with you to deliver you, says the Lord. Then the Lord extended his hand and touched my mouth, saying, See, I place my words in your mouth! This day I set you over nations and over kingdoms, to root up and to tear down, to destroy and to demolish, to build and to plant (Jer 1:4–10).

In this first point of contrast we learn how perfectly the infinite God accommodates Himself to His creatures. In every vocation, God deals with the human person in accord with that person's nature. Never forcing it beyond its powers, He yet gives it the grace to say "yes" to Himself. Neither bruising nor hurting, God dealt with the sensitive soul of the youthful Jeremiah in a sensitive way.

The second point of contrast is had in the prophet's reply. Here there is no eager "Here I am; send me!" Rather, we find the timid, diffident "Ah, Lord God! I know not how to speak; I am too young" (1:6). This was no outright refusal of the divine request; it was simply an avowal of his own inadequacy of which he was most conscious. Modern society would likely call Jeremiah an introvert, hesitant, because of his sensitiveness, to go out into the world and proclaim a message it did not want to hear. He would have much preferred to stay at his family home in Anathoth, just a couple miles to the northeast of Jerusalem. Here he could have grown in his personal love of God, pondering the word of God as spoken by others.

But God chose Jeremiah to speak that word himself. And it is only when we understand the personality of this man that we will appreciate the courage it took to fulfill that task. The "confessions" of Jeremiah (11:18—12:6; 15:10-21; 17:12-18; 18:18-23; 20:7-18) should be read for an intimate glimpse into the soul of the prophet. There we discover how much his vocation really cost him.

Woe to me, mother, that you gave me birth! a man of strife and contention to all the land! I neither borrow nor lend, yet all curse me. Tell me, Lord, have I not served you well? Have I not interceded with you for my enemies in the time of their misfortune and anguish? You know I have. Remember me, Lord, visit me, and avenge me on my persecutors. Because of your long-suffering banish me not; know that for you I have borne insult. When I found your words, I devoured them; they became my joy and the happiness of my heart, because I bore your name, O Lord, God of Hosts. I did not sit celebrating in the circle of merrymakers; under the weight of your hand I sat alone because you filled me with indignation. Why is my pain continuous, my wound incurable, refusing to be healed? You have indeed become for me a treacherous brook, whose waters do not abide! (Jer 15:10–18).

Nonetheless, it was this man whom God chose to bear prophetic witness to Judah's fall and to the end of one phase of the Old Testament story.

JEREMIAH AGAINST THE NATIONS

But do you gird your loins; stand up and tell them all that I command you. Be not crushed on their account, as though I would leave you crushed before them; for it is I this day who have made you a fortified city, a pillar of iron, a wall of brass, against the whole land; against Juda's kings and princes, against its priests and people. They will fight against you, but not prevail over you, for I am with you to deliver you, says the Lord (Jer 1:17–19).

Jeremiah against Judah's kings and princes! Against its priests and people! Certainly no one would have predicted that the timid, introspective youth from Anathoth would ever have stood up in righteous anger against a fellow citizen, much less against a member of the royal court or the king himself. But Israel's God was unique and unique were His dealings with His people. To appreciate these dealings we must study the situation that provoked the call of Jeremiah. Briefly, it was moral and religious corruption. He tells his listeners to search carefully throughout the city of Jerusalem and see if they can find just one person "who lives uprightly and seeks to be faithful" (Jer 5:1). They will search in vain. For the people swear falsely and commit adultery; they "grow fat and sleek" as "they go their wicked way" (Jer 5:27–28).

Moreover, they have forsaken the Lord Himself, "the source of living waters," and, in seeking out the false gods, "they have dug themselves cisterns, broken cisterns, that hold no water" (Jer 2:13). The fathers, the children and the women of Jerusalem work together to prepare the sacrifices for the pagan goddess (Jer 7:18). They have even defiled the Lord's own house by setting up their abominable idols in it (Jer 7:30). And the barbaric practice of human sacrifice has been introduced into the religion of God's people (Jer 7:31). These crimes, both moral and religious, are horrible enough. But there is a familiar ring in the recounting of them. Injustice, impurity, idolatry and superstition—were these not the same sins against which Amos and Hosea, Isaiah and Micah had preached so vigorously? Perhaps the names of the gods were different now, and the method of defrauding the poor more sophisticated. But basically the perversion was the same. What, then, was unique about the situation that brought forth a Jeremiah at God's word?

It is one of the characteristics, and one of the great glories, of Israel's prophets that they saw every crime as unique, just as they saw every evidence of God's hand as sign of a unique intervention. The here and now of *this* sin had a horrible reality about it that fell full force upon the prophet and made his mind reel at the thought of it. This was no abstract notion to be neatly tabulated under the category of "sin." This was the deliberate action of a flesh-and-blood Israelite raising his clenched fist defiantly against the Lord.

Unless we can appreciate the totality with which the prophets entered into the situation of their day, we will never appreciate the vehemence of their denunciations or the genuineness of their pleading. And in this, every prophet of Israel was unique. In this, we can learn a lesson from them. Among us it happens so frequently, unless and until we are called back to the reality of sin, that sin becomes a commonplace. It is something we learn gradually to live with, to accept as easily as we do a broken rung in a ladder. At times the sin is even given religious status by being practiced in the name of religion. This is the depth of perversion. Israel had reached this depth.

It is true that the opposition to the individual sinners seems to be more clearly marked in Jeremiah. This is partly because the prophet's unusual sensitivity provoked in him a sharper outcry. But also we are favored with much more detailed information in Jeremiah's case than in that of Isaiah or the others. Baruch, the prophet's secretary, has served us well with his accounts of the prophet's activities, of his sufferings and of his spiritual battlings with the people and with the Lord.

Let us now see how this man from Anathoth stood up against those who would disown their God. The most precious object of veneration for the people of Jerusalem and of all of Judah was the temple. And rightly so. Did it not rival, if not in size, at least in splendor, some of the great temples of the pagan world? Was not the liturgy that was celebrated here most inspiring both by reason of its profound religious meaning and by reason of the perfection of its execution? And above all, did not the invisible Lord of heaven and earth dwell within the walls of this sacred building in some mysterious way? Aware of all this, Jeremiah could yet stand at the gates of this house of God and threaten the people with its utter destruction. "Put not your trust in the deceitful words: 'This is the temple of the Lord! . . .' I will do to this place which I gave to you and your fathers, just as I did to Silo" (Jer 7:4. 14). So did God speak about the temple through His prophet.

We must understand the popular conviction about the temple

to appreciate their horrified reaction to these words. The temple was more than just a place of worship; it was the symbol of God's protection of His people. It had become the superstitious guarantee of survival. Looking on its massive walls they felt secure and smugly complacent. Jeremiah's words burned through the rubble of this false security and smug complacency and touched the heart of the temple's meaning:

Only if you thoroughly reform your ways and your deeds; if each of you deals justly with his neighbor; if you no longer oppress the resident alien, the orphan, and the widow; if you no longer shed innocent blood in this place, or follow strange gods to your own harm, will I remain with you in this place, in the land which I gave your fathers long ago and forever (Jer 7:5–7).

From chapter 26 we learn that this temple speech caused a popular uprising against the prophet that almost ended in his death. Jeremiah's calm assurance to them that he spoke God's word, not his own, shamed them into letting him go. But the experience did not stay his attack on sin. One day he took some of the civil and religious authorities outside the city. There he solemnly announced the destruction of that magnificent city sitting so proudly on its mountain height. To give added punch to his announcement he brought forth an earthen flask and smashed it before their eyes: "Thus says the Lord of hosts: Thus will I smash this people and this city . . . " (Jer 19:11).

For this Jeremiah was scourged and imprisoned overnight (see Jer 20:1–3). But again, it did not stay his accusing tongue. Even the king himself was not immune. One of the prophet's strongest indictments was against Jehoiakim, one of the last kings of Judah (609–598). Jeremiah accused him of gross injustice, of setting his eyes and his heart "on nothing except on your own gain, on shedding innocent blood, on practicing oppression and extortion" (Jer 22:17). These are strong words to be spoken to any man. Jeremiah directed them to a king! The whole passage in 22:13–19 should be read for an appreciation of the seriousness of the prophet's charges.

On another occasion Baruch had put down, at Jeremiah's dictation, all the oracles uttered by the prophet since his call (see Jer 36). He then went, in Jeremiah's place, to the temple and read the oracles to the approaching worshippers. Consternation resulted. The scroll was taken to the king. Then, as one of the secretaries read the oracles, the king reached up and cut off each section of the scroll as it was read and tossed it into the fire. It was an expression of his supreme contempt for the man of God and his message. But the man of God and his message were both to outlive Jehoiakim. After the burning of the original scroll, Jeremiah dictated his oracles yet another time. It is this second dictation that forms the basis of our present book of *Jeremiah*.

In this prophet, then, we have a remarkable illustration of the power of God's call. Because it is He who calls, there is always the assurance of great things accomplished, despite the frailty of the one who is called. Man need only respond with what is in his power; God supplies what is lacking.

Lo, I am summoning all the kingdoms of the north, says the Lord; each king shall come and set up his throne at the gateways of Jerusalem, opposite her walls all around and opposite all the cities of Juda. I will pronounce my sentence against them for all their wickedness in forsaking me, and in burning incense to strange gods and adoring their own handiwork. But do you gird your loins;

115

stand up and tell them all that I command you. . . . They will fight against you, but not prevail over you, for I am with you to deliver you, says the Lord (Jer 1:15–17a. 19).

JEREMIAH AND THE NEW COVENANT

The doctrine of election goes far in explaining the meaning of the Old Testament: God *chose* Israel to be His people. Not for any merits of their own had He taken them to Himself, but solely as an act of His own free choice. "For you are a people sacred to the Lord, your God; he has chosen you from all the nations on the face of the earth to be a people peculiarly his own. It was not because you are the largest of all the nations that the Lord set his heart on you and chose you, for you are really the smallest of all nations. It was because the Lord loved you . . . " (Deut 7:6–8).

But the divine election was not something that was just expressed and then ignored. It had to be expressed in a concrete form, in a relationship that had its own rules and regulations and ways of living. In the case of Israel the divine election was expressed in the form of a covenant. Covenant was a common expression of relationship in the ancient world. It could be a pact between two friends, such as David and Jonathan, involving equal obligations on both sides. Or it could be between a superior and an inferior. Among the examples of this type we know of the covenants made by ancient Hittite emperors with vassal kings subject to them. In this case the vassal alone bound himself to certain obligations which he met out of loyalty to the emperor who had saved him from his enemies. In most cases the covenant was sealed in some ritual form, such as the sacrifice of an animal or common partaking of food.

The covenant that expressed the relationship between God and Israel most closely resembled that between the Hittite emperior and his vassal kings. Israel, too, bound herself to certain obligations (the Ten Commandments are a summary of them) out of loyalty to Yahweh who had brought her out of the land of Egypt. The continued protection of God could be expected. "If you keep my law, I will be your God and you will be my people" is a capsule summary of the covenant between God and Israel. If we have repeated here observations already made in an earlier chapter, it is felt that the review is helpful for a deeper appreciation of Jeremiah's contribution to covenant theology.

The history of Israel is the history of that covenant. While there were times of fervent love on Israel's part, and while she raised up some great men of God, the history as a whole was not one of fidelity to the covenant. As we have seen throughout our study of the prophets, she failed, and at times failed miserably. The prophets were called by God precisely for this reason, to restore in Israel the sense of covenant, or, as Hosea put it so beautifully, to bring a faithless bride back to her spouse.

Israel's failure, in the prophets' thinking, could mean only one thing: the end of divine protection. And this is what they preached. Defeat, destruction, exile would be the fruits of disobedience. The northern kingdom experienced its doom in 721 B.C. at the hands of the Assyrians; the southern kingdom would soon suffer its own at the hands of the Babylonians. Jeremiah himself would live through it and so witness the fulfillment of his words. But was this to be the end of the story? Had God intervened in history for this? Had He made His plan of salvation so dependent on one people that, if they failed, His plan would be completely frustrated? The prophets saw at once how

117

ridiculous this was. That is why they also foretold a return of Israel from exile, a new intervention of God's that would make secure His plan. Isaiah, we saw, spoke of the messianic prince who would rule His people with justice in those days.

Jeremiah also foresaw this return. The entire chapter 31 deals with it. Here the prophet emphasizes the powerful hand of God coming down to save His people much as He had saved them in the land of Egypt. But Jeremiah adds a new thought. The chapter reaches a climax in the solemn prediction of a new covenant. Let us read the words of the prophet:

The days are coming, says the Lord, when I will make a new covenant with the house of Israel and the house of Juda. It will not be like the covenant I made with their fathers the day I took them by the hand to lead them forth from the land of Egypt; for they broke my covenant, and I had to show myself their master, says the Lord. But this is the covenant which I will make with the house of Israel after those days, says the Lord. I will place my law within them, and write it upon their hearts; I will be their God, and they shall be my people. No longer will they have need to teach their friends and kinsmen how to know the Lord. All, from least to greatest, shall know me, says the Lord, for I will forgive their evildoing and remember their sins no more (31:31–34).

Our Lord alluded to these words of Jeremiah when, at the Last Supper, He spoke of the new covenant sealed in His blood which would be shed for the remission of sins. He thereby announced to His followers that the solemn oracle of Jeremiah was fulfilled. Jeremiah, of course, had no idea that his words would be fulfilled in such a way. This would have been far beyond his comprehension. And yet the prophet's words were an important link in the chain of revelation that led to Jesus Christ. True, he still pictured the covenant in the same terms as the old one, a covenant between God and the people of Israel and Judah. And there is no hint here (nor would we expect it 600 years before Christ) of the almost incredible way in which the covenant would be sealed, through the passion, death and resurrection of the Son of God.

But there is this. Jeremiah sees the new age as a period when God's law will be written upon the hearts of men. What does this mean? It means that God's law will not be seen as some external force that binds man to minute observations just because they are written down in these words. Rather, it will be an inner law of freedom that expresses itself in an almost automatic love of God. In the new age, man will do God's will, not because it is written in the book, but because he loves God, he "knows" the Lord with the intimacy of personal experience. The meaning of this becomes clear in the fulfillment. As Christians who have witnessed the lengths to which God would go to prove His love for us, we have every reason to make a spontaneous return of that love to God. "No longer will they have need to teach their friends and kinsmen how to know the Lord."

St. Paul grasped the meaning of Jeremiah's "new covenant" when he spoke of the Mosaic Law as a tutor, or as a nursemaid that leads the child to school. "But now that faith has come, we are no longer under a tutor" (Gal 3:24–25). Christ has made it possible for us to love God with a love that knows no need of external law. "All, from least to greatest, shall know me, says the Lord . . ."

Such an oracle could only have been evoked by the conviction that Israel had failed to keep her part of the covenant. Jeremiah realized this. He also realized that there was a weakness in the covenant of old that the new one would have to overcome. This weakness was the covenant's vulnerability, the fact that it could be vitiated in whole by the sins of individuals. In the passage immediately preceding the words quoted above, he refers to a proverb that states that children could suffer for the sins of their parents: "The fathers ate unripe grapes, and the children's teeth are set on edge" (31–29). In these words were the sufferings of those in exile seen as punishment for the sins of an earlier generation.

Such a thing will not happen in the new age to come. God's covenant with His Christian people will never be placed in jeopardy by the sins of individuals. This covenant will last forever and will bring salvation to all who freely give themselves to it. If there are sinners, and sinners there will be, God will deal with them individually: ". . . through his own fault only shall anyone die . . ." (31:30). As for those who turn to God He will "forgive their evildoing and remember their sins no more" (31:34). The new covenant will truly be an "everlasting covenant" attesting forever to the love of God for man.

JEREMIAH'S CONTRIBUTION
TO REVELATION

Aggiornamento is an important word in the Church today. Everyone has heard of it, but not all know what it means. Literally we could call it "updating" or "adaptation to the present day." In the religious context in which it is used, it means making the truths of Christianity intelligible and meaningful for contemporary man. This should not be as startling an idea as it may sound. It does not mean that there is no absolute truth, or that the truths of Christianity are constantly being revised to accommodate new philosophical opinions or scientific discoveries. While it is true that the appearance of such accommodation is given at times, further study shows that such is not the case.

We have an excellent and often used illustration of the principle in the story of creation as narrated in the opening chapter of *Genesis*. When the theory of the gradual evolution of created nature gained ascendancy and the evidence for it came close to certain, the Church expressed her willingness to accept it and admitted that no biblical truth was thereby placed in jeopardy. For the fundamentalist, however, the biblical truth of a creation in a period of six days was involved and any compromise of this truth would be an outright attack on the Bible's inerrancy. What the fundamentalist fails to see is that, while truth cannot change, its formulation and manner of presentation can. The ancient biblical author wanted to teach that God created everything. He presented this truth in the form of a six-day work week and a seventh day of rest. His simple, uneducated readers could understand the truth better in this way because it pictured the rhythm of their own week of labor and rest. The Church still teaches the same truth, but she presents it differently than did the ancient priestly author because her children are scientifically more sophisticated and, in terms of work weeks, differently oriented. The truth has not changed, but its presentation has. This is one form of *aggiornamento*.

If all of this is true we might ask why we are so concerned with what Jeremiah or any of the prophets had to say. They spoke over 2500 years ago, at a time when people were much less sophisticated and, for the most part, not even literate. What would appeal to them is not likely to appeal to us. A stronger argument can be found in the observation that Jeremiah's book is part of the *Old* Testament, in a sense where "old" is more than a temporal reference. It is the old in contrast to the new, to the perfect revelation of the Father realized in the Son. What does Jeremiah, who spoke before Christian fulfillment had taken place, have to say to *me,* a Christian?

There are several answers. The most easily understood, perhaps, is that the realities of the Old Testament revelation, inasmuch as they were prefigurings or foreshadowings of the realities of the New, make the latter the more intelligible. Jesus' words at the Last Supper about the new covenant of His blood take on fresher meaning when seen against the background of Yahweh's covenant with Israel and of Jeremiah's oracle about a new covenant, even granting the prophet could not see the reality he was describing with the eyes of Christian fulfillment. It can be affirmed, indeed, that there is hardly a verse of the New Testament that could not be enriched in meaning through a clearer understanding of the Old Testament.

Sharing in the nature of this same answer, but seeing it in more profound dimensions, is the organic unity of biblical revelation, the inner continuity between Old and New. The revelation of the past is not some static uncovering of abstract truth but a dynamic penetration of the meaning of contemporary history in a way that brings out the sharing of that history and of that revelation in a unifying pattern. The pattern continues on into the New Testament; it is not broken by Jesus Christ but is *fulfilled* in Him. Here it reaches a climax that makes clear what was only dimly revealed, brings to fulfillment what had already been promised. It is because of this essential and organic continuity, then, that the realities of the Old take on greater significance. It is not merely a superficial unity of expressions, of social or cultural conditions, but an inner, dynamic unity of a plan that is as deeply involved in Jeremiah's protests as it is in the sermons of Jesus of Nazareth. Unless we understand the role of Jeremiah's protests, we will never fully understand the role of Jesus' sermons.

An example will help. Before Jeremiah's time, there was a strong emphasis on the people of God as a community. God had saved Israel, not an individual person. It was through the community that the individuals came to know and to worship Yahweh. It was impossible to think of the individual save in the context of the community. It was a good emphasis, one that we today would do well to grasp more surely and one which the Church is trying to foster in her liturgical renewal.

But the idea could be over-emphasized. It could be thought that the individual does not count at all, that his destiny is completely dissolved in the destiny of the community. Although there are evidences of a more balanced view even in the ancient period, there is also evidence of exaggeration. There were cases in Israel where, if one member of a family committed a crime, the entire family was punished (see Jos 7:2–26). At the time of Jeremiah, a proverb was making the rounds that sounded the discontent felt by reason of this conviction of the way of God's justice: "The fathers ate unripe grapes, and the children's teeth are set on edge" (Jer 31:29). But no one was better qualified to interpret God's justice than Yahweh, and he denied the complainers' major by declaring firmly that ". . . through his own fault shall anyone die; the teeth of him who eats the unripe grapes shall be set on edge" (Jer 31:30).

Jeremiah, of course, like the people, was thinking of the distress presently afflicting the nation. The affliction was being attributed to the sins of a former Israel, and Jeremiah insisted that his contemporaries had sins enough of their own to explain any punishment they were receiving. In saying this Jeremiah intended no denial of the social or community nature of God's plan of salvation. It is still through the people of God that the saving acts of God are manifested. But he had provided a needed boost to a concept that would figure largely in Ezekiel's ministry and would reach its climactic term in the Christian conviction of full personal freedom and individual responsibility as developed by St. Paul. This developing manifestation of God's saving will, therefore, reveals the unity and continuity in God's revelation. But it is only by appreciating the depths of Jeremiah's involvement that the revelation is had.

But there is still one more lesson that Jeremiah can teach us. It is the lesson of contemporaneity. This is something like *aggiornamento,* but with an added twist. We have seen how Jeremiah spoke out against the sins of his day. They are the familiar ones of injustice, impurity, lack of charity, superstition, idolatry. Men of God had spoken out against these before Jeremiah; men of God are still speaking out against them today. The prophet offers nothing fresh in this regard.

Also, the reasons he gives for reform had been given before. God has brought you out of the land of Egypt and given you your land and your independence. Serve him out of gratitude for His love and out of loyalty to the covenant He has made with you. Serve Him or you will perish. Although the Christian motives for avoiding sin are basically the same, love of God and fear of His punishment, those motives have much greater impact because of Jesus Christ. And so in this matter, too, Jeremiah offers nothing we do not already have.

Yet there is a spirit in Jeremiah's preaching that is most important for us today. It is a spirit of involvement, of being one with his people, of sympathy and compassion, of anguish and torment felt for others, with others and because of others. His words still ring with this aliveness, this reality of encounter between himself and his contemporaries. This is why we call it a spirit of contemporaneity. It is a spirit that identifies oneself with those to whom the good news of salvation is being brought. *Aggiornamento,* whereby we present Christian truths in a modern form, is important. But it is not enough. We must also make *ourselves* contemporary. Jeremiah did this in an exceedingly perfect way. Reading his words in faith and humility we, too, will catch this spirit of contemporaneity.

7.

ZEPHANIAH, NAHUM, HABAKKUK

ZEPHANIAH AND THE DAY OF THE LORD

OUR next prophet brings us down almost a half century after the ministry of Isaiah. Zephaniah, we are told in the opening verse of his prophecy, received the word of the Lord "in the days of Josia, the son of Amon, king of Juda." We know that Josiah instituted a great religious reform after he ascended the throne in 640 B.C. There is no indication of such a reform in our prophet's few chapters. He must have preached, therefore, around the middle of the century. He had a lot to preach about. After the death of Hezekiah in 687 B.C., a king who had at least made an effort to do God's will, Judah suffered under the reign of the thoroughly corrupt Manasseh and Manasseh ruled from 687 to 642 B.C. For some forty-five years Jerusalem witnessed more pagan practices than at any time in her history (see 4 Kgs 21:1–18). It was at the climax of this period the Zephaniah appeared on the scene.

Judah, of course, was still vassal to Assyria. Despite the many plots that had been hatched among the subject nations to throw off her yoke, Assyria continued to rule. And Manasseh, like the others, acknowledged the sovereignty. This included paying some kind of homage to the gods of Assyria. While Assyria doubtless would have been satisfied with a token acknowledgement, Manasseh went all out. He erected pagan altars in the temple of Jerusalem, restored throughout Judah the local shrines that had been destroyed, at least partially, by Hezekiah because of the sins committed there, caused divination and magic to flourish and even introduced the barbarous practice of human sacrifice.

Did Manasseh and the people who followed him consciously reject Yahweh? Probably not, and this is what made the situation even worse. Over the years so many pagan practices and false notions had crept into the national religion that many of the simple people could not distinguish the good from the evil, the false from the true. The true religion had been overlaid with a hard thick crust of paganism. Possibly, Manasseh justified his actions. Baal and all the other gods—were they not members of Yahweh's court? This, then, would justify their worship and the introduction of the barbarous and obscene rites that were part of that worship. In the face of these the strict morality of Yahwism gradually gave way. Corruption, violence and injustice were the "new morality."

We cannot paint the religious picture too black. And if we do not paint it black enough we shall fail to understand the stirring words of the prophets and fail to appreciate the enormity of their task. That Israel, as a people, survived all the changes in world politics during those thousand years before Christ can be called a miracle. If so, then it is a far greater miracle that Old Testament religion survived all the abuses it suffered at the hands of Israel. The prophets are principally responsible for this miracle.

Zephaniah contributed his part to the miracle. The particular means he used was a theme that we already found in Amos, some 150 years before. It is the theme of "the day of Yahweh."

We can recall that Israel looked forward to the time when God would come in judgment, when he would come to save Israel and destroy her enemies. It was called the "day of the Lord." Amos had been the first to come out quite bluntly and tell them that the day they looked forward to would be a day they would rue, for it would be a day of destruction and doom for Israel. "Prepare to meet your God," Amos had cried out in menacing tones to his audience.

Zephaniah goes even further. In some detail he describes what the day of the Lord will be. He does it with some of the bitterest irony to be found in the Old Testament, rivaled in this respect only by a few of his fellow prophets. He first creates the attitude of holy expectation. They must be silent. The Lord is coming in glory. There will be a feast, of course, as any celebration must be when the Lord is present. But *this* is a "slaughter feast," one in which punishment and not reward will be meted out.

Silence in the presence of the Lord God! For near is the day of the Lord, yes, the Lord has prepared a slaughter feast, he has consecrated his guests. On the day of the Lord's slaughter feast I will punish the princes, and the king's sons, and all that dress is foreign apparel (1:7-8).

Notice that the prophet does not condemn the king, evidently the young Josiah, who genuinely regretted the evil of Manasseh's reign and hoped to restore pure religion. Rather, it is the "princes, and the king's sons, and all that dress in foreign apparel" who are the object of condemnation. These are the court officials, a sort of royal "cabinet" that Josiah had inherited from his predecessors. Their pro-Assyrian sympathies extended even to an imitation of foreign clothing.

But this does not exhaust the prophet's thoughts on the day of the Lord. He goes on in a ringing crescendo, giving new glimpses into the horror of that day. A climax is reached when he cries out,

A day of wrath is that day, a day of anguish and distress, a day of destruction and desolation, a day of darkness and gloom, a day of thick black clouds, a day of trumpet blasts and battle alarm against fortified cities, against battlements on high (1:15–16).

We recognize in these words the inspiration for the medieval hymn that now forms the sequence of the Solemn Requiem Mass.

We must not forget that these outbursts, expressive of such profound feelings, were not born in a vacuum. They are the responses of a sensitive spirit to a reality either within or without. The greater the outburst, the greater must be the reality that provoked it. The haunting power of Zephaniah's words, therefore, helps us to realize the ugliness of the sin he witnessed.

Throughout most of the short prophecy it would seem that Zephaniah's condemnation is total. Yet he is not without his words of hope. They are not as explicit, perhaps, as Isaiah's oracles concerning the ideal prince. But in one way they go further inasmuch as they identify more surely those who are to be saved. They are "the humble of the earth, who have observed his law" (2:3). The Hebrew word used here for "humble" became a technical expression in a later period for a special group within Israel, the group of those who knew oppression in this world but who also knew the special favor and love of God. Originally, the word simply meant one who was poor. Then it came to mean anyone who suffered because of human injustice. It was such as these who would experience, according to Zephaniah, divine justice on the day of the Lord: "Seek the

Lord, all you humble of the earth, who have observed his law; seek justice, seek humility; perhaps you may be sheltered on the day of the Lord's anger" (Zeph 2:3). (Incidentally, it is with this group of "humble ones" with whom Mary is identified in the beautiful hymn of the *Magnificat:* see Lk 1:48–52.)

As in *Isaiah,* so too here we meet the oracles against the nations: "For Gaza shall be forsaken, and Ascalon shall be a waste, Azotus they shall drive out at midday, and Accaron shall be uprooted. . . . He will stretch out his hand against the north, to destroy Assyria; he will make Ninive a waste, dry as the desert. . . . Is this the exultant city that dwelt secure; that told herself, 'There is no other than I!' How has she become a waste, a lair for wild beasts? Whoever passes by her hisses, and shakes his fist!" (Zeph 2:4–13–15). As we also saw in *Isaiah,* this type of oracle was greatly developed in a later period. It seems that this has happened here also. But it is not always easy to know how much was added. What is more important is that the passage reflects the same profound theology as do all the oracles against the nations: whoever thwart the divine plan, whether they be gentiles or chosen people, will be punished.

In the third chapter our prophet returns to the main theme: the day of the Lord and His chosen people. Here the city of Jerusalem, that place of God's special presence, the highly favored city of David, becomes the symbol of the people. She is "rebellious and polluted, . . . she hears no voice, accepts no correction" (3:1–2). "Therefore," the Lord cries out to her, "wait for me . . . against the day when I arrive as accuser" (3:8).

These are the stinging words of prophet against people. Read carefully the first 8 verses of this chapter. Notice the absoluteness of the charge and the certainty of the punishment. Then notice the shift of tone beginning in verse 9. Here the prophet views the conversion of the people to God and their eventual restoration. It is certain that Zephaniah did not speak all the words of this chapter on the same occasion. Some think he did not speak these final words at all; they were added after the exile, when the punishment had been executed and the people converted. It is possible, but not necessary. It is possible that the prophet himself, in his later life, would have developed the idea he already expressed in 2:3. This hope of the prophet would then have been given explicit formulation by a later editor who made his additions when the hope had been realized:

From beyond the rivers of Ethiopia and as far as the recesses of the North, they shall bring me offerings. . . . At that time I will bring you home, and at that time I will gather you; for I will give you renown and praise, among all the peoples of the earth, when I bring about your restoration before your very eyes, says the Lord (Zeph 3:10–20).

NAHUM, HABAKKUK AND THE JUDGMENT OF GOD

"Men involved" is the way in which we described the prophets of the Old Testament. Neither attic recluses nor starry-eyed visionaries, they were men immersed in the history of their times, realists for whom all reality has a God-directed meaning. If we can capture this spirit of the prophets, we have understood them well. One of the most forceful and most frequent expressions of this realism was the prophetic denunciation of people and nation, the calling down in vivid terms of God's judgment on His chosen people as much as on their enemies. We have seen this characteristic in Amos and Micah, in Isaiah and Jeremiah, and even in Hosea, the prophet of divine love.

It would seem that this prevalence in the prophets of the God of judgment is somewhat strange, especially when we realize that the first and most important notion that Israel had of God was that He was a *saving* God. And the message of the prophets was a part of *salvation* history. Why, then, all this emphasis in the prophets on judgment and condemnation? It is history that provides at least part of the answer. Perhaps if Israel had been able to live on her own tight little island, secure from all external influences, alone with her God and with her divine directives, things might have been different. But God wanted Israel to grow with history, to learn to see Him and His saving activity in the events of history. In this way would their commitment to God in faith be perfected in historical reality and not in an unreal world. In this way would they best prepare for the Son of God who would dwell completely in our midst, becoming like to us in all things save sin.

In a way, this was a divine gamble. This subjection of Israel to all the forces of history could lead to her contamination by the evil in history. But even from this good could be drawn. Here, too, man would learn more of God. Free to obey or disobey, man would know both salvation and judgment. This is the great lesson Israel learned. And most of the learning took place in the period of the monarchy, when she particularly encountered the evil forces and partially succumbed to them. Is it any wonder that the prophets were raised up in this same period to ensure that Israel learned her lesson well?

The two prophets, Nahum and Habakkuk, are both prophets of divine judgment. Both lived in approximately the same period and both are almost completely unknown except for their oracles. This, as we have seen more than once, is the way of prophets; it is God's story, not their own, which they came to announce. Nahum's announcement is not difficult to interpret. The opening verse tells us it is an "oracle about Ninive," and the rest of the book confirms this by depicting the coming fall of Assyria's capital city. The subject is not new. Amos, Isaiah, Jeremiah and others had their oracles against the nations. And Assyria, destroyer of the northern kingdom and savage scourge of the ancient world for almost 300 years, was the hated foe of Israel and her God and the chief object of the prophetic oracles. That the three chapters of Nahum's prophecy should be confined to an exultant description of Assyria's imminent destruction is not too surprising.

How can we explain this "holy glee" over the fate of another nation, even if it is pagan and an enemy? The divine condescension is part of the answer. This means simply that God did not make Christians out of the Old Testament people. Only with the full revelation of God in His Son and with His supreme example of love would men be enabled to love their enemies, do good to those who hate them (Matt 5:44). But there is more than this. In the concrete way that the prophets had of thinking and of expressing themselves, the Assyrians were the personification of sin. Since they were enemies of God's people, they were enemies of God. And to rebel against God is to sin. It was the conviction, therefore, that these cruel warriors were living symbols of evil that provided much of the fire for the prophetic denunciation.

One of the joys of reading the description of Nahum lies in discovering his vivid recapturing of the sound and fury of battle:

133

The crack of the whip, the rumbling sound of wheels; horses a-gallop, chariots bounding, cavalry charging, the flame of the sword, the flash of the spear, the many slain, the heaping corpses, the endless bodies to stumble upon! (3:2–3).

It is hard to imagine that this came from anyone who was not in the thick of it himself.

But notice, too, how the same prophet sees the horror of war and pictures it in graphic terms:

Emptiness, desolation, waste; melting hearts and trembling knees, writhing in every frame, every face blanched! (2:11).

Even this, however, does not diminish the prophet's joy at the defeat of this ancient foe. With gladness in his heart he addresses the fallen Assyrian:

There is no healing for your hurt, your wound is mortal. All who hear this news of you clap their hands over you; for who has not been overwhelmed, steadily, by your malice? (3:19).

Nahum's prophecy must have been delivered at a time when the Assyrian collapse was close at hand. The growing power of Babylonia, which was to be the instrument of that collapse, was there for all to see. The time, therefore, would have been shortly after 650 B.C., perhaps in the reign of Josiah (640–609), making the prophet a contemporary of the great Jeremiah.

It is not as easy to pinpoint the period of Habakkuk's prophecy, although it would have been in the same general period as Nahum's. It depends on the interpretation of his message. Like Nahum, he tells us nothing about himself. But unlike Nahum, he makes no explicit reference to the people or person whom he is describing. Some think the prophet is condemning the Assyrians, as Nahum did. Or it may be the Chaldeans (see 1:6), also known as the Babylonians, the pagan people that destroyed Assyria and that was ultimately to destroy Jerusalem in the not too distant future. In either case, the meaning of the condemnation would be basically the same as in Nahum's oracle. These are enemies of God and of God's people; God's judgment will come down upon them.

It may be, however, that Habakkuk is denouncing his own nation of Judah, in particular the Egypt-loving faction that controlled the country after Josiah's death in 609 B.C.:

Destruction and violence are before me; there is strife and clamorous discord. This is why the law is benumbed, and judgment is never rendered: because the wicked circumvent the just; this is why justice comes forth perverted (1:3–4).

When we read these lines, it is as though we were in the world of Amos again, or of Isaiah. They are lines that would have had meaning for the people of God. If this is true, then we can see in verses 5–6 that God is calling up "Chaldea, that bitter and unruly people," to be the instrument of His anger against Judah. Notice once again how completely convinced these prophets were that nothing happens without the Lord's bidding. If Chaldea is indeed to take Jerusalem, it could only be because the Lord "raises him up."

But the prophet realizes that there are the righteous, too. Destruction, God's judgment, must come; the sins of the wicked demand it. For

the rash man has no integrity; but the just man, because of his faith, shall live (2:4).

The words would be made famous when St. Paul would use them again with a fuller and richer meaning. Life, which ultimately means life with God, is obtained only by a firm commitment to that God, a complete giving of oneself. This alone guarantees absolute assurance in time of sorrow.

Like all the prophets, Habakkuk was utterly dismayed by sin, by the acts of rebellion against the sovereign God. In fact, the dismay must have been even more keenly felt in him. It evoked from his heart a terrible cry that opens his entire prophecy:

How long, O Lord? I cry for help but you do not listen! I cry out to you, "Violence!" but you do not intervene. Why do you let me see ruin; why must I look at misery? Destruction and violence are before me; there is strife, and clamorous discord. This is why the law is benumbed, and judgment is never rendered: because the wicked circumvent the just; this is why judgment comes forth perverted. Look over the nations and see, and be utterly amazed! For a work is being done in your days that you would not have believed, were it told (1:2–5).

This is bold language. A creature questions the creator about His actions. It can only be explained by the prophet's revulsion at the reality of sin. The cry is a tribute both to Habakkuk's own sensitivity to evil and to the infinite patience of God. Sin cries out for vengeance, but God awaits repentance. Judgment and punishment are only the last resort.

We are tempted to think of these two prophets, and especially of Nahum, as chauvinists glorying in the destruction of the nation's enemy. We have already offered a theological basis for this apparently radical nationalism and an explanation, founded on the incomplete nature of revelation, for the prophetic emphasis. But we would also do well to note that a comparison with the parallel pagan literature would, in many cases, expose the relative restraint of Israel's authors. The Canaanite literature, to which the third chapter of *Habakkuk* is indebted for much of its rich imagery, is especially filled with gory details which our authors have, for the most part, eschewed. Moreover, we must not judge Nahum too strictly on the sole basis of what has been preserved of his oracles. The canonical content of his prophetic ministry may well be an indictment of his disciples or of his later editors who expressed their own brand of nationalism by their choices. Taken out of a possibly larger context, the oracles could reveal a boldness and bluntness they did not originally have.

8.

EZEKIEL

THE CALL OF EZEKIEL

EZEKIEL is probably the most difficult of all the prophets to understand. His love of symbolism and rich imagery overpower the ordinary imagination and make one wish that God had chosen a less "complicated" man as His prophet. But difficult as his language is, Ezekiel does make some sense if we have the historical background in mind. He might have been different in many ways, but he was as much a man of his times as any prophet.

Ezekiel bridges the period between the time of Josiah and the exile in Babylon. It was a period of uncertainty for Judah and of a rapid growth in power by Babylonia. In 597 B.C. Nebuchadnezzar, the Babylonian general, made an assault on Jerusalem and carried away many captives. Ezekiel was one of them. The city itself still had ten years of grace before it would come to an ignominious end, destroyed by the Babylonian hordes. The deportation in 597 of some of the leading citizens was a sign of things to come.

It is impossible that Ezekiel would not have known of Jeremiah. The latter had gained notoriety during the reign of Josiah (640–609), and during the reigns of the following kings he continued to stir up much religious dust. Likely Ezekiel, of a priestly family as was Jeremiah, was only a youth when he was taken captive, but he would have been old enough to recognize the prophetic character of the older man of God. He may even have heard him preach in Jerusalem.

As a prophet, Ezekiel began his preaching while in exile and continued until some time after the destruction of Jerusalem. The latest date given in the book itself (29:17) is the twenty-seventh year of Jehoiachin or 571 b.c. The book, edited at a later date by disciples, is at least logical in the order of its presentation of oracles. There is no scurrying from one period to another and back again. After the description of the opening vision (chs. 1-3) his book contains a series of oracles delivered during the first period of his exile and which were intended to prepare his fellow Israelites for the coming destruction of Jerusalem (chs. 4-24). Then comes a section containing oracles against the nations (chs. 25-32). A message of hope for his fellow exiles delivered after Jerusalem's fall (chs. 33-39) is finally followed by a detailed vision of the new Jerusalem (chs. 40-48). Thus, it is possible to divide the book into very distinct sections that do follow one another in some kind of order.

Like Isaiah and Jeremiah, Ezekiel has preserved for us the account of his own vocation. He tells us that he was living among his fellow Jewish exiles "by the river Chebar," that is, near one of the large artificial canals that the Babylonians had constructed to bring the water of the Euphrates River to the surrounding areas. This particular settlement of exiled Jews was to the southeast of the great city of Babylon. All the evidence indicates that the exiles were not badly off. They lived in separate settlements, but were given a great amount of freedom, allowed to gather for discussions and celebrations and to practice their own faith.

139

Since sacrifice could only be offered in the temple of Jerusalem, here they could only gather for prayer meetings, a form of worship that was continued later on in the synagogue services. Ezekiel probably conducted some of these services in exile.

The Jews were surrounded by an immense amount of culture. Not too far away was Nippur, the ancient religious center with two thousand years of religious culture behind it already. And to the northeast was the imposing city of Babylon, one of the great wonders of the ancient world. The walls surrounding it were five miles in length and wide enough to accommodate a chariot. Inside, the buildings and temples and palaces were unlike anything the Jewish exiles had seen and must have made them stare in wonder when they visited this pagan city. No doubt some of the Jews were so overwhelmed by this splendor that they quickly forgot what they had left behind at the other end of the Fertile Crescent. There is evidence that many became active in the commercial life and gradually assimilated themselves into the local population. Some of these, too, were so impressed by the imposing cult of the Babylonians that they abjured their Jewish faith and worshipped pagan gods.

But Ezekiel was not concerned with these. There were many others who retained the faith of their fathers and even became more confirmed in it by suffering. Their only desire was to return to Jerusalem where they could worship God again in fitting sacrifice. Psalm 137 (136) should be read to appreciate the intensity of their longing for Jerusalem. So strong was this hope in fact that in some it took on fantastic proportions. It was expected that God would soon step in and bring an end to this Babylonian domination, that Jerusalem would be spared and the exiles returned home. False prophets rose up and fanned these dreams to a white-hot intensity. Jeremiah had to preach against them in Jerusalem and the Babylonian police put two of them to death for sedition (see Jer 29:20–22).

This was the atmosphere both in Jerusalem and in exile when Ezekiel received his call: "There the hand of the Lord came upon me" (1:3). The inaugural vision is reported in the first three chapters. The first of these reports the scene of God's apparition. It is like nothing else in the Bible. It is a remarkable illustration of the divine accommodation to a man possessed of a strongly developed imagination. The vision comes from the north in the midst of a storm cloud and accompanied by lightning flashes, all of which brings out the majesty of what is occurring. The vision involves a four-part picture with both human and animal heads and members. Moving here and there, sparkling like bronze, full of eyes and with wheels within wheels, the vision is a manifestation of God's indescribable spirit. Above all this was a firmament, stretched out "like glittering crystal." And over this was a throne "looking like sapphire." Upon it was one "surrounded with splendor. . . . Such was the vision of the likeness of the glory of the Lord" (1:26–28).

Throughout this detailed and even fantastic scene, one truth is brought home above all others. It is the utter majesty of the transcendent God. It is a truth worthy of frequent meditation. We can never forget that the God who communicates so generously with His creatures is still the infinite Lord, the completely holy God, the absolute master of nature and of history. Ezekiel was overcome by this majesty and glory and described it in the only way he could. Paul could do no better when he described himself being "caught up to the third heaven" (see 2 Cor 12:1–4).

141

It is not until the second chapter that we come to the actual message of the vision. It is only here that we learn that Ezekiel is called to preach to the rebellious Israelites. The very adjectives used to describe them show that these are not words of consolation he must preach. A scroll was unrolled before the prophet, and the scroll was filled with writing: "Lamentation and wailing and woe!" (2:10). This was to be the content of the prophet's message. Obviously, Israel still had not learned her lesson. Even the initial punishment of exile had not brought her to her senses. She was still committing the same old sins of a false confidence in the inviolability of the city of Jerusalem. Her cup of suffering needed filling, and Ezekiel was to convince her that it would be filled.

It is one of the unique features of the biblical prophets that they are never dead instruments of God's prophetic gift. They are not lifeless computers storing up the divine message for later use when God's spirit comes once more upon them and pushes the correct button. The prophets react, and often in a vehement form. We have seen how Isaiah expressed his eagerness to be sent by God. And we read of Jeremiah's intimate plea that he be excused because of his youth. In other words, God chose real men, men who were completely honest and who responded with their whole being. Ezekiel was no exception. And, as He always did, God accommodated Himself to the peculiar nature of His prophet and indicated Ezekiel's mission in a highly symbolic form. He was told to eat (in vision, of course) the scroll on which the divine message was inscribed.

"Son of man, he then said to me, feed your belly and fill your stomach with this scroll I am giving you. I ate it, and it was as sweet as honey in my mouth. He said: Son of man, go now to the house of Israel, and speak my words to them" (3:3–4). Unlike Jeremiah, Ezekiel felt no hesitation about going out and speaking words of "lamentation and wailing and woe." For Ezekiel these words were "sweet as honey" in his mouth; they were the Lord's words. Such was the call of the prophet Ezekiel as he dwelt among the exiles in Babylon.

EZEKIEL AND THE DOOM TO COME

Was Ezekiel a cataleptic? This is a question frequently asked by the scholars because of certain of his actions as described in his book. At one time there would have been a horrified reaction to the suggestion. Surely a man of God could not be a cataleptic or border on psychic abnormality! The reaction was that of a generation that lived perpetually in a defensive atmosphere, when religion was derided and the Bible was catalogued along with the pagan legends of the ancient Near East. That day has passed. No longer is there any need to fear a full scientific approach to the Bible. We know there can be no contradiction between God's truth as found in nature and as found in His inspired word. Moreover, the world in general is better prepared to accept religious values, to see the hand of God in the abnormal as well as the normal. There is no need, therefore, to make a special effort to hide what might be considered defects in the history of religion. The objective person realizes that a defect is often accompanied by a special gift, and he will admire the gift all the more.

So it matters not whether Ezekiel was a cataleptic or whether he tended to psychic abnormality. We cannot know for sure whether either is true. We do know that almighty God used this man's peculiar characteristics to further His mission. That mission was to warn the Jewish exiles that Jerusalem was doomed and that there would be no salvation in the near future. Let us take a look at the many ways in which Ezekiel got this message across.

First of all, he was seized by the spirit of God and placed in the midst of the exiles of Tel Abib in Babylonia, while the huge and complicated vision of the glory of the Lord went clanking off (see 3:12–15). For seven days the prophet "sat among them distraught," perhaps in some form of cataleptic stupor. It was the first of a series of signs to the people, this one simply bringing home to them the reality of the prophet's presence in their midst. In the next sign (4:1–3), Ezekiel was told to take a clay brick and draw on it the picture of a city (Jerusalem) in siege. Holding an iron plate between himself and the besieged city, the prophet represented God and His iron determination not to interfere with the city's doom.

Next, he was to lie on his left side for 390 days and on his right side for forty days, the former period representing (by some unknown symbolism) that of the northern kingdom's exile, and the latter that of the southern kingdom's. His bared arm against Jerusalem represented God's powerful will to punish (4:4–8). His eating and drinking in small quantities, and of unclean food, symbolized the starvation diet of the future exiles (4:9–15). His hair and beard (considered of great dignity by the ancient Semites) were to be shaved off and divided into three equal parts. The first part was to be burned, the second to be cut with a sword and the third to be scattered abroad (5:1–4). Thus were the different fates of the conquered citizens of Jerusalem depicted.

All of these signs were seemingly performed one after the other. They must have had a great effect on those who witnessed them. The ancient peoples had a great appreciation for symbolism, something which we, unfortunately, because of our great concern for *scientific* truth, have lost. Perhaps the reading of the prophet Ezekiel with a sympathetic ear will help us to regain this precious gift.

There were other signs, stranger yet to our unimaginative mentalities. Ezekiel was to dig a hole through the mud-brick wall of his house and pass through it as one driven off into exile. This would be the fate of the citizens of Jerusalem (12:3–16). Again, he must eat and drink as though shaken with fear and trembling to indicate the mental state of those in a siege (12:17–20). He must even perform a sword-dance in a spirited rhythm as a prophecy of the slaughter to come (21:13–22).

Jeremiah had been commanded not to marry and have children. His virginity was a warning to Jerusalem that it, too, would be without sons or daughters (Jer 16:1–4). Ezekiel is now asked not to perform all the mourning services for his deceased wife. It was a difficult request because she was "the delight of his eyes," and the ancient Semites were accustomed to elaborate mourning rites. But it was to be a lesson to the others that the "death" of Jerusalem would be so overwhelming that they would not think even to mourn (24:15–27). We cannot be sure of the manner in which all of these signs were carried out by the prophet. And it would be useless to attempt to reconstruct the physical reality. What we can be sure of is that the message was made plain. And it came from a man of God who represented God in the midst of His people.

In the very beginning of his ministry Ezekiel was reminded, in

PROPHETS OF SALVATION

strong terms, of the urgency of his mission. He was appointed "a watchman for the house of Israel" (3:17). As watchman, his task was more than simply noting the approach of disaster; it was to bring the news to all. So important was this that if a wicked man failed to forego his evil deeds because the prophet had failed to warn him, then the prophet would be responsible for the resulting death. In all cases, the actions of the people were to be judged in part by the faithfulness of Ezekiel to his post:

If I say to the wicked man, You shall surely die; and you do not warn him or speak out to dissuade him from his wicked conduct so that he may live: that wicked man shall die for his sin, but I will hold you responsible for his death. If, on the other hand, you have warned the wicked man, yet he has not turned away from his evil nor from his wicked conduct, then he shall die for his sin, but you shall save your life. If a virtuous man turns away from virtue and does wrong when I place a stumbling block before him, he shall die. He shall die for his sin, and his virtuous deeds shall not be remembered; but I will hold you responsible for his death if you did not warn him. When, on the other hand, you have warned a virtuous man not to sin, and he has in fact not sinned, he shall surely live because of the warning, and you shall save your own life (3:18–21).

An important development is had here in the conception of the prophetic office. His task is not only to bring God's word to the people but to act as shepherd and guide to his people. To be sure, this is already contained, to some extent, in the office of spokesman for God, but the office could be interpreted in a purely mechanical sense. Ezekiel's words bring out more clearly than ever before the sense of pastoral responsibility that must be felt by the prophet.

But a much more discussed point in Ezekiel's teaching is touched on in this passage and then developed at some length in

146

chapter 18. It has to do with the question of responsibility for sin. To understand the discussion we must first say a word about the concept of corporate solidarity and, consequently, of corporate responsibility. The consequence noted here is not a necessary one, but it was drawn frequently, especially in primitive society. The ancient Israelite, like his neighbor, looked upon himself as tied in an intimate bond to his ancestors, especially to the eponymous ancestor from whom the various families in a clan or tribe are descended. In particular were the bonds between the members of the same family so strong that what one did was bound to influence the others. This was carried over into the realm of criminal responsibility as is evident in the case of the vendetta, where other members of the family or tribe could suffer for the crimes of one.

In Israel's oldest literature we also find evidence for a notion of individual responsibility. Each one is responsible for his own crimes and must suffer for them. The notion that others could also suffer for these same individual crimes lived on in Israel for a while, but not with the tenacity that it did among other more primitive peoples. The case of Achan, whose entire family is put to death for the crime of the father, is an exception (Jos 7:16–26). We can be fairly sure that by the time of Ezekiel this was no longer a commonly held conviction. The prophet, then, is not introducing in chapter 18 a new concept of individual responsibility.

To understand Ezekiel's point, we must appreciate the situation to which he directed his oracle. First of all, it was the case of the *nation,* not an individual, suffering. Secondly, as Barnabas Lindars has pointed out in a study on this chapter (*Vetus Testamentum,* XV, 4, pp. 452–467), a distinction must be made be-

147

tween criminal responsibility and divine retribution. In the first case, we begin with a definite crime committed and then determine who is to be punished and to what extent. In this case, all Israel would agree that he who committed the crime must suffer. In the second case, we begin with a situation of prosperity or woe, trace this back to God's pleasure or displeasure and then determine what was the crime, or sin, that brought on the displeasure (in case of the presence of woe).

It is this second case that is applicable here. Israel finds herself in the presence of woe; the present generation is suffering. Obviously, divine retribution is at work. But who is responsible? It was commonly held that a nation's sins could be visited on future generations, even though it was agreed that each individual must suffer for his own crime. In other words, the divine wrath was conceived to have been stored up over several generations and to have been poured out on a particular one far beyond its own culpability. This is the meaning of the proverb they were quoting: "Fathers have eaten green grapes, thus their children's teeth are on edge" (18:2).

It is this very precise notion, then, that Ezekiel denies when he states: "As I live, says the Lord God: I swear that there shall no longer be anyone among you who will repeat this proverb in Israel. For all lives are mine; the life of the father is like the life of the son, both are mine; only the one who sins shall die" (18:3–4). He has made use of the language of individual responsibility, that of "father" and "son," and applied it to the generations of Israel. The present generation of Israel is suffering for its own sins, and none has the right to claim that divine retribution is being extended over a number of generations.

In fixing the teachings of Ezekiel on this point, we must be careful not to have him say more than he does. He is not, for example, denying the concept of divine retribution altogether. Nor does he deny the concept of corporate solidarity, the conviction of belonging in a real sense to others within the same group. As in the case of all the prophets, his teaching is occasioned and conditioned by the very real situation in which he lived. His message is that Jerusalem must fall and the people, who still remain behind, be taken into exile. And this is for the sins of the *present* generation, not for some generation of the past. They have no valid complaint against the Lord. But Ezekiel, as we shall see, could also speak words of salvation when those words were needed.

EZEKIEL AND SALVATION

. . . thus says the Lord God: See, I am coming at you! I will inflict punishments in your midst while the nations look on. Because of all your abominations I will do with you what I have never done before, the like of which I will never do again (5:8–9).
For thus says the Lord God: I myself will look after and tend my sheep. . . . I will rescue them from every place where they were scattered when it was cloudy and dark. . . . I will bring them back to their own country and pasture them upon the mountains of Israel. . . . The lost I will seek out, the strayed I will bring back, the injured I will bind up, the sick I will heal . . . shepherding them rightly (34:11–16).

In these two passages from Ezekiel we have beautifully expressed the double message of the prophet, a contradictory message on the face of it, one of punishment and doom and one of salvation and comfort, both directed to the historical Israel. What makes eminent sense of the paradox is, of course, the historical background. The first message is part of a series of oracles (chs. 4–24) delivered while Jerusalem was still standing and the people still confident that nothing could happen; here the prophet warned them in clear terms that their fate was sealed. The second message belongs to a different series (chs. 33–39), proclaimed after the fall of Jerusalem in 587 B.C. and assuring the exiles that God had not abandoned them altogether. But just the bare statement of this changing historical background is hardly enough to understand the exultant cry of hope that springs from the prophet's heart. We must get inside Israel herself, experience with her the fall of her great city and the deportation into Babylonia of the majority of her people. Moreover, we must experience this, to the best of our ability, with an appreciation of all the background of Israel herself, with her convictions about her God and His relationship with His people. Only then will we really open our hearts to this great prophet of the exile.

Yahweh was the one true God, the sole creator of everything that was, and the sole master of all history's unfolding. But Yahweh was also Israel's God in a most special way. He had chosen the people freely from among all the nations of the world, nations much more powerful than Israel, and had entered into convenant with them, binding Himself, in return for their loving loyalty, to protect them and to be their God. As with the people, so with the land. It was the land promised by God to their ancestors and the promise had been fulfilled. It was the object of Yahweh's concern and the place of His special presence. It was, in fact, a holy land. And endowed with a special measure of this holiness was the holy city of Jerusalem, the place "which the Lord, your God, chooses out of all your tribes and designates as his dwelling" (Deut 12:5).

This was Jerusalem, the mount of Sion, to the people of Israel. While we would not justify, at least we can understand a bit more clearly, the conviction of the people that Jerusalem was inviolable. It was God's dwelling place and no army was mightier than God. A little more than a hundred years before, about 701 B.C., the great Assyrian general Sennacherib had laid siege to the city and threatened to destroy it. By God's grace, however, the Assyrians were unable to carry out their threat and Jerusalem was spared (see 2 Kgs 18–19). The experience could only have made the people still more convinced of the inviolability of their holy city.

And now, in 586 B.C., that holy city lay in ruins, the walls destroyed, the palace and the temple of the Lord put to the torch. The glory of the people was no more. "By the streams of Babylon we sat and wept when we remembered Sion. . . . May my tongue cleave to my palate if I remember you not, if I place not Jerusalem ahead of my joy" (Ps 137 [136]:1.6). So went the plaintive words of a psalm composed in exile by one who tasted keenly the bitter ashes of complete dejection and despair. This spirit we must appreciate if we want to feel, as the exiles must have felt, the shock of Ezekiel's new message from the Lord. Instead of doom, he now preached salvation; instead of warning, hope. And again he does it in his inimitable way, in imagery and allegory that convey the message in a way that few prophets could match.

He begins his new words of God by recalling a theme that Jeremiah had developed in his prophecy, the theme of the false shepherds (see Jer 23:1–2; 25:34–38). They are the rulers of the people and the ones responsible in a special way for the welfare of their people (see Ez 34:1–6). But instead, God's sheep "have been given over to pillage . . . for lack of a shepherd, because my shepherds did not look after my sheep, but pastured themselves and did not pasture my sheep . . ." (Ez 34:8). But now God will intervene directly: "I myself will look after and tend my sheep" (34:11). And then in due time, "I will appoint one shepherd over them to pasture them, my servant David; he shall pasture them and be their shepherd. I, the Lord, will be their God, and my servant David will be prince among them. I, the Lord, have spoken" (34:23–24). Ezekiel, too, shares the hope of the future Messiah, as did Isaiah and Jeremiah before him. He describes him, as Jesus of Nazareth would later describe Himself, as the shepherd of His people, the one shepherd of the flock.

The most famous of Ezekiel's visions of restoration and salvation is that of the dry bones (ch. 37). The prophet is led by the Lord, in vision, to a vast plain where before him is a huge number of dry bones, bones picked clean of all flesh, disconnected and scattered about. The bones represent the lifeless people of Israel who, utterly dejected by their fate, had been saying "Our bones are dried up, our hope is lost, and we are cut off" (37:11). The vision gains in power if we keep in mind that for the ancients one of the greatest misfortunes was to remain unburied. It was felt that, unless the body was placed in a burial place, there would be no rest for the departed. Thus Ezekiel's vision was a picture of Israel deprived of the spirit of life, for all intents dead to the world, but not even granted the grace of a decent burial.

It was over these dry bones that the word of the prophet, which was the word of God, was to be spoken. "Dry bones, hear the word of the Lord!" So the Lord commanded, and so His prophet spoke: "I prophesied as I had been told and even as I was prophesying I heard a noise; it was a rattling as the bones came together, bone joining bone" (37:4–7). After this, he was told to

152

prophesy again and to command the spirit of life to come into the restored bodies. "I prophesied as he told me, and the spirit came into them; they came alive and stood upright, a vast army" (37:10). The whole vision, of course, is a prophecy of Israel's eventual restoration, of her return from exile and of her new beginnings in the land of promise. The vision of the dry bones would remain one of the classic pieces of inspired literature, a testimony, not so much to Israel's imaginative genius, as to her faith in a God who can bring life to the dead.

Like those of the other prophets, Ezekiel's vision of the future was on the grand scale, and it was always in some way connected with the present that provided the theme and the imagery of the future hope. This means, first of all, that he saw the future not as a series of well-spaced events gradually unfolding but as one glorious and climactic divine intervention. Thus, when Israel's return from exile is described, there is pictured at the same time the perfect peace and prosperity she would enjoy. In reality there could be and would be long periods of time between the successive fulfillment of the vision.

The second observation, that the picture of the future hope is colored by the prophet's own age, is brought out most clearly in the final nine chapters (chs. 40–48). The prophet describes the new age as characterized by a new Temple, a perfect Temple which would be the center of the new Israel's new life. And all the tribes would have their allotted dwelling places around this building. The description is clearly patterned on much of Israel's historical past, but above all on the Temple of Jerusalem. For the exiles it was the loss of the Temple that had hurt most. Its rebuilding would be one of their first concerns on returning home. What better figure could Ezekiel use to climax his message

153

of salvation than the picture of a new Temple in a new city. And "the name of the City shall henceforth be 'The Lord is here'" (48:35).

Ezekiel has been called, not without justification, the "father of Judaism." By this is meant that he was the main figure responsible for the flourishing, in the post-exilic period, of that priestly concern for law and ritual holiness that marks the period. We know that when the Jews did return to Judah and Jerusalem after the decree of Cyrus, they took with them a burning desire to restore the past and to assure its continuation by a rigid adherence to the law. This desire and concern were manifested in the final shape given to the Pentateuch, now commonly known as Torah. And Israel became the people of the book, the people of the Law.

To designate Ezekiel as father of this community is perhaps attributing too much to a single influence. For a priestly circle existed that was responsible for similar emphasis. It would be better to say that Ezekiel was the principal figure of that circle, for his priestly interests and concerns are evident throughout his prophecy, notably in the concluding chapters. What is more distinctive of Ezekiel is that he was a true prophet who worked in the great prophetic tradition. Never before in Israel's history had these two parallel movements been so intimately associated as in this one great figure of the exile. By their union in him the two were assured of even greater esteem in the eyes of God's people for all time to come.

154

9.

SECOND ISAIAH

PROPHET IN EXILE

"SECOND Isaiah" is a strange name for a prophet. "Isaiah II" would be a bit more acceptable, but it might suggest, falsely, that this man is the other prophet Isaiah's son. The name "Second Isaiah" has been given by the biblical scholars to a prophet whose name we do not know but whose prophecies were connected, in a late period of Old Testament history, with the prophecies of the true Isaiah to form one book.

For a long time this editorial work went unsuspected. It was thought that the historical Isaiah (who, as we saw, lived about 750–680 B.C.) wrote the whole book. A closer examination of the Hebrew vocabulary, of the style and of the contents, however, made it very clear that the same man could not have written all of these chapters. In fact, several hands were seen to have contributed to our book. First, there is the historical Isaiah responsible for the majority (but not all) of the first 39 chapters. Then there is our "Second Isaiah" who was responsible for chapters 40 to 55 at least. And many scholars think that chapters 56 to 66 were written by still another prophet (or prophets), called, as you might suspect, "Third Isaiah."

All this dividing is not done without reason. It is clear, for example, that chapters 40 to 55 concern a period of history about

150 years after the historical Isaiah; we will see this shortly. And one of the observations we have so emphatically made about prophets is that they were *men of their times*. The Isaiah of the eighth century had no consuming interest in what would happen in the sixth century. Why, then, would he have written about it? The answer is, of course, that he did not. But this answer raises another question. Why were these oracles combined in one book under the same heading? There are several facets to this answer. First of all, the Jewish people of that time had no hesitation in combining in one book the contributions of various authors. We already saw this when we studied the prophet Isaiah; the books were not so much the property of individual authors as the literary and religious heritage of *Israel*. Hence combinations of the kind found here were readily made when it was felt that there was a close similarity of teaching, or a particularly conspicuous continuity in historical development and revelation. Most of the books of the Old Testament are compilations of this kind. Our present book is a notable example. Perhaps the Bible scholars showed little imagination in calling the author of chapters 40 to 55, "Second Isaiah," but it does get a point across.

What was the situation faced by our anonymous man of God? The people of Jerusalem and Judah were still in exile in Babylon. Ezekiel had spoken his last word of encouragement and hope about 570 B.C. It was now some 25 years later, about 545 B.C. The world situation was changing rapidly. All the news reports in Babylon those days were filled with references to a great Persian soldier named Cyrus. He had already conquered vast territories to the east, north and west of Babylonia. The king of Babylon was sitting on an uneasy throne, and he knew it!

It was just at this time that one of the greatest voices of the Old Testament was raised up among the exiles in Babylon. This messenger of God saw all the great historical events as manifestations of the omnipotent Lord. His indomitable faith in the power of God led him to draw unforgettable pictures of the absolute divine control over nature:

Who has cupped in his hand the waters of the sea, and marked off the heavens with a span? Who has held in a measure the dust of the earth, weighed the mountains in scales and the hills in a balance? Who has directed the spirit of the Lord, or has instructed him as his counselor? . . . Behold, the nations count as a drop of the bucket, as dust on the scales; the coastlands weigh no more than powder. . . . Before him all the nations are as nought, as nothing and void he accounts them. To whom can you liken God? With what equal can you confront him? (40:12–18).

And to make clear that he is speaking to men of his own day about events that involve them, he addresses an oracle in the Lord's name to the Persian king himself, who would be the Lord's instrument for the liberation of His people:

Thus says the Lord, your redeemer, who formed you from the womb: I am the Lord, who made all things, who alone stretched out the heavens; when I spread out the earth, who was with me? . . . It is I who confirm the words of my servants, I carry out the plan announced by my messengers; I say to Jerusalem: Be inhabited; to the cities of Juda: Be rebuilt; I will raise up their ruins. . . . I say of Cyrus: My shepherd, who fulfills my every wish; he shall say of Jerusalem, "Let her be rebuilt," and of the temple, "Let its foundations be laid" (44:24–28).

The necessary complement to this unshakable faith in the one God was an absolute abomination of the false gods of Babylon or of any people. In one of the greatest satires ever composed against idols, our prophet describes in detail how the pagan carpenter takes a piece of lumber and throws half of it in the fire to warm himself and uses the other half to make himself a god before whom he prostrates himself, crying out, "Rescue me, for you are my god" (44:6–20). And again, to make clear that he is speaking of the gods of the pagan city in which the exiles find themselves, he speaks of them by name:

Bel bows down, Nebo stoops, their idols are upon beasts and cattle; they must be borne up on shoulders, carried as burdens by the weary. They stoop and bow down together; unable to save those who bear them, they too go into captivity (46:1–2).

This unconditioned acceptance of one God was implicit in Israel's faith from the beginning; here it is stated with a clarity and a conviction never before witnessed. And it is this faith of "Second Isaiah" that gives character to his message. It is because of his absolute conviction regarding the supremacy and lordship of Yahweh that he can speak so forcefully and challengingly to his compatriots. What he says is designed to interpret the recent victories of Cyrus and to bring a new heart to a despondent people.

"Comfort, give comfort to my people, says your God" (40:1). These are the first recorded words of the prophet; they must have fallen on unbelieving ears. Even the anonymous man of God himself admits that, from one point of view at least, there is little reason to take comfort. He knows that far-off Jerusalem "has no one to guide her of all the sons she bore; she has no one to grasp her by the hand, of all the sons she reared! . . . Desolation and destruction, famine and sword! Who is there to comfort you? Your sons lie helpless at every street corner like antelopes in a net. They are filled with the wrath of the Lord, the rebuke of your God" (51:18–20).

158

.Yet he dares to offer this comfort. And he even spells out, as he must if he will gain any hearers at all, the terms of the comfort: "A voice cries out:'In the desert prepare the way of the Lord! Make straight in the wasteland a highway for our God! Every valley shall be filled in, every mountain and hill shall be made low; the rugged land shall be made a plain, the rough country, a broad valley" (40:3-4). To the exiles these were, indeed, words of comfort. They spoke of return to their homeland, of the Lord's leading them out through the great Syrian desert that separated them from Sion, of the end of exile. Because it was to be the Lord Yahweh's doing, the event is described with the magnificence and splendor worthy of the Lord. Language becomes the vehicle for the description, not primarily of the historical, but of the theological reality, the truth of the divine intervention.

What determined the Lord's decision? The prophet was told that Jerusalem's "service is at an end, her guilt is expiated; indeed she has received from the hand of the Lord double for all her sins" (40:2). In the prophetic view, sin is the cause of suffering, and suffering removes the guilt of sin. Israel's crimes had been expiated; she could now return home. Easily enough said, but how was this to be accomplished? The people, while they may have accepted the prophet's word that the Lord would do this, did not expect Him to come down like a giant warrior and lead them personally through the desert. They understood the figurative language of the prophet well enough. As in the past, God would use His chosen instruments to carry out His purpose.

The remarkable thing here is that the instrument was to be the pagan general, Cyrus. "Thus says the Lord to his anointed, Cyrus, whose right hand I grasp, subduing nations before him, and disarming kings, and leaving the gates unbarred. . . . For the sake of Jacob, my servant, of Israel my chosen one, I have called you (that is, Cyrus) by your name, giving you a title, though you knew me not" (45:1–4). This is how "Second Isaiah" has interpreted the fateful events that led this Persian soldier to be poised at the crossroads of history, waiting to give the final blow to the Babylonian Empire. The prophet's interpretation was to be proven true, his words of comfort spoken with authority. In the year 539 B.C. Cyrus took Babylon, and one of his first official acts was to issue a decree permitting the exiled Jews to return to their homeland. The pagan prince fulfilled the words of God spoken by the prophet: "He shall rebuild my city and let my exiles go free without price or ransom, says the Lord of hosts" (45:13).

Much of the imagery used by the prophet to describe this liberation is taken from the ancient traditions that described the exodus from Egypt. It is said that the Lord "opens a way in the sea and a path in the mighty waters" (43:16), a clear allusion to the crossing of the Red Sea. "In the desert I make a way, in the wasteland, rivers" (43:19), he continues; "they did not thirst when he led them through dry lands; water from the rock he set flowing for them; he cleft the rock, and waters welled forth" (48:21). There is a profound lesson in this use of traditional imagery. The prophet establishes thereby a connection between the event of the past, the exodus from Egypt, and the present event, the return from exile. The latter is a new exodus, another climactic saving act of God that is part of the whole divine plan. The plan, revealed initially in the freedom from slavery in Egypt, is revealed more clearly in the freedom from slavery in Babylon. The resumption of the language and figures of old teaches us that there is a continuity in history that is intended by God and completely under His direction.

The exodus from Babylon was not to be the final exodus. There would be another one in the future, a spiritual exodus from the slavery of sin and death, this time accomplished by another saving intervention of God's in the person of His Son. When the New Testament writers describe that saving event, they, too, show the continuity of the one grand plan of God by using the language of old to describe the new. The words of "Second Isaiah" are taken up again and given a fullness of meaning by reason of the fullness of the plan (see, for example, Is 40:3 and Lk 3:4–5).

THE SUFFERING SERVANT

One day, several years after the first Pentecost Sunday at the beginning of the Christian era, a royal minister of the Queen of Ethiopia was riding in his carriage on his way back to his native country. He had been to Jerusalem in order to worship there the one true God. He had with him a scroll containing part of the Jewish Scriptures. At the time he was reading this passage from the book of Isaiah: "He was led like a sheep to slaughter; and just as a lamb dumb before its shearer, so did he not open his mouth . . ." (Acts 8:32–33). At that very moment Philip, one of the first Christian deacons, appeared and asked the minister if he knew the meaning of what he was reading. The minister answered, "Why, how can I, unless someone shows me?" And he asked Philip if the prophet was speaking of himself or of someone else. "Then Philip opened his mouth and, beginning from this Scripture, preached Jesus to him" (Acts 8:34–35).

161

This incident in the life of the early Christian community teaches us the great importance the Church saw in this passage; it was used as the beginning of Philip's preaching. Throughout the history of Christianity, the readers of the Bible have asked, like the Ethiopian minister, "Of whom is the prophet speaking?" And the Church has always answered, with Philip, that the words are spoken of Jesus who "was led like a sheep to slaughter." The Church, of course, answers from the fullness of revelation. She understands the fullness of the divine intention in the prophetic words. But to see how God prepared for this fulfillment we must go back, with the scholars, to the Old Testament period when the words were first spoken. The answer will not be as clear then as it was after Jesus' coming. But seeing the vision with the dimness of the prophet himself will help us to appreciate the clarity of the vision in the time of fulfillment.

The passage that the minister was reading was part of a long poem in "Second Isaiah" (52:13—53:12). It is one of four poems in the same book, all of which speak of the "Servant of Yahweh." The poems are: 42:1-9; 49:1-13; 50:4-9; 52:13—53:12. All of these should be read separately, as individual poems, since they were originally composed separately and later put in the book as we now find them.

Our anonymous prophet, as we saw, lived towards the end of the exile, brought comfort to his fellow Jews by the prediction of an imminent return to the homeland and uttered some remarkable oracles on the power of the one God. But he is as well known for these four poems which describe the Servant of Yahweh and which reach their magnificent climax in the description of the Servant's suffering for the sins of others. Since we have insisted so much on the fact that the prophets were men of their time, we must ask what these poems meant to the people in exile. They were not written just for Christians who were to come more than 500 years later. In the first poem (42:1–9) we learn that God's Servant is to bring God's law, God's justice, to the whole world. He will do this, not by loud shouting or by force, but by kindness and by justice to all. It is possible that the prophet is thinking of Israel herself here, who would return home and there, by living a new life with God, would show the nations the light of the divine law.

Here is my servant whom I uphold, my chosen one with whom I am pleased, upon whom I have put my spirit; he shall bring forth justice to the nations, not crying out, not shouting, not making his voice heard in the street. A bruised reed he shall not break, and a smoldering wick he shall not quench, until he establishes justice on the earth; the coastlands will wait for his teaching (42:1–4).

In the second poem (49:1–13), the power of God acting through the Servant is emphasized. The Servant himself would meet with much opposition in bringing God's truth to the world, but God would see to it that even kings and princes would bow before His Servant:

Thus says the Lord, the redeemer and the Holy One of Israel, to the one despised, whom the nations abhor, the slave of rulers: when kings see you, they shall stand up, and princes shall prostrate themselves because of the Lord who is faithful, the Holy One of Israel who has chosen you (49:7).

Note how the concept of suffering has been subtly introduced, and how this has been used as a means to extol the power and the glory of God. Note, too, that the Servant is specifically called Israel here: "You are my servant, he said to me, Israel, through whom I show my glory" (v. 3). But, while our prophet had the

163

people of God in mind as the instrument of God's climactic revelation, he probably also saw Israel as symbolic of another Servant of the future.

The third poem (50:4-9) develops the note of suffering which the Servant must endure in carrying out his task. Despite the maltreatment, he remains faithful to God who continues to uphold him. While Israel could again be had in mind here (she suffered much in exile), the notion of an *individual* Servant seems emphasized. Perhaps the prophet himself was gaining a clearer notion of God's ultimate plan for the salvation of all peoples.

I gave my back to those who beat me, my cheeks to those who plucked my beard; my face I did not shield from buffets and spitting. The Lord God is my help, therefore I am not disgraced; I have set my face like flint, knowing that I shall not be put to shame (50:6-7).

The last poem (52:13-53:12) is the longest and most beautiful of all. The prophet's thoughts have reached a level of clarity and of conviction not present in the earlier poems. The Servant is described as undergoing unparalleled suffering, and, most important, as suffering for the guilt of others:

He grew up like a sapling before him, like a shoot from the parched earth; there was in him no stately bearing to make us look at him, nor appearance that would attract us to him. He was spurned and avoided by men, a man of suffering, accustomed to infirmity, one of those from whom men hide their faces, spurned, and we held him in no esteem. Yet it was our infirmities that he bore, our sufferings that he endured, while we thought of him as stricken, as one smitten by God and afflicted. But he was pierced for our offenses, crushed for our sins; upon him was the chastisement that makes us whole, by his stripes we were healed. We had all gone astray like sheep, each following his own way; but the Lord laid upon him the guilt of us all. Though he was harshly treated, he submitted and opened not his mouth; like a lamb led to the slaughter or a sheep before the shearers, he was silent and opened not his mouth. Oppressed and condemned, he was taken away, and who would have thought any more of his destiny? (53:2–8).

He is spoken of, too, as being "cut off from the land of the living" (53:8–9), which most Christian interpreters have understood as a reference to his death. The following verses, then, would refer to his restoration to life by God and to an eternal reward:

If he gives his life as an offering for sin, he shall see his descendants in a long life, and the will of the Lord shall be accomplished through him. Because of his affliction he shall see the light in fullness of days; through his suffering, my servant shall justify many, and their guilt he shall bear. Therefore I will give him his portion among the great, and he shall divide the spoils with the mighty, because he surrendered himself to death and was counted among the wicked; and he shall take away the sins of many, and win pardon for their offenses (53:10–12).

When we read this magnificent poem with its detailed picture of torment and suffering, we can understand why the early Christians would have described the passion of Our Lord in a terminology that was borrowed, to a great extent, from our anonymous prophet of the exile. Why should they not have used his phrases? As one interpreter puts it, the poem reads as though it had been written at the foot of the cross on Calvary. But more important than the words are the ideas contained in the poem. In the other poems it was announced that the Servant must suffer, but it was not clear *why* he must suffer. If the Servant *was* Israel, then Israel must suffer for its own sins, an idea that was not new to the chosen people. Here it is explicitly stated, and several times (see 53:4–6.9–12), that he is suffering for the sins of others. This is *vicarious* suffering and is a completely new idea in the Old Testament. It would, it is clear, add great depth to the rich theology of suffering that would reach its climax in the New Testament. Our anonymous prophet had prepared the way very well for the later Christians to understand what Jesus Christ had done for them.

Another new idea that we find in these Servant of Yahweh poems is the role he will have in the conversion of the nations. The Hebrew people of the Old Testament did not ordinarily give too much thought to God's concern for the pagans. Since these worshipped false gods they looked upon them as God's enemies. Only rarely, as in *Genesis* 12:3, do we find some hint that the pagans, too, could be the object of a divine blessing, and there it is mentioned only to underscore the blessing of Abraham. This narrow nationalism had become so marked in the period after the exile that one inspired author, with remarkable vision, was moved to compose a special book to oppose this mentality. We know it as the book of Jonah, and are accustomed to placing it among the prophets. But in our overwhelming interest in the extraordinary events related in the book we fail completely to understand its message. The author writes of a man of God who was called by God to bring His word to the Assyrian people, that they might be converted and do penance for their sins. Since the Assyrians were the greatest enemies of Israel's past history (they no longer existed as a nation at the time of the book's composition), Jonah reacted in a manner typical of his contemporaries. He wished to have no part in bringing God's word to God's enemy. The greater part of the book, then, brings out the universal character of the divine concern and how that concern overcomes all odds in fulfilling its purpose. This is the spirit and the message of the book of Jonah.

"Second Isaiah" preceded the author of the book of Jonah by some years, and he had the same conviction. He, however, envisions the Servant of Yahweh bringing the news of salvation to the gentiles. Before his time, it was ordinarily God Himself who was described as establishing His reign over all the world (see Is 9:6). Now the Servant will perform this role:

It is too little, he says, for you to be my servant, to raise up the tribes of Jacob, and restore the survivors of Israel; I will make you a light to the nations, that my salvation may reach to the ends of the earth (49:6).

Our unknown prophet gave depth to the theology of universal salvation by his depicting of the figure of the Servant.

The relationship of the Suffering Servant to the royal Messiah described by Isaiah and Jeremiah is difficult to determine. Surely our prophet knew of this other figure. He knew, too, that there was something valid about the figure. But he also had come to know that royal pomp and glory are passing things in God's sight; they were not essential for God's purpose. Suffering, he had learned, can be even more important. If asked what kind of Messiah he looked forward to, he would likely have answered that it was a suffering Messiah.

Despite his anonymity, "Second Isaiah" contributed much to our spiritual heritage. His concept of the mighty Lord of nature and of history is unsurpassed. His message of comfort, even though given originally to a group of exiles, still has meaning for us who can read in it the great God's concern for all men. Above all, his picture of a Servant of God who could suffer for others, even for all peoples of the world—this *must* be his greatest contribution. We can be extremely grateful to those faithful Jews who cherished this prophet's oracles and preserved them for all Christian readers.

10.

POST-EXILIC PROPHETS

WE now enter a completely new phase of Old Testament history and of revelation. It is Haggai and Zechariah, the first prophets of the post-exilic period, who usher in the new period. The very first verse of each of their books tells us that they received the call to speak God's word in the second year of the reign of Darius; it was 520 B.C. What was the situation? For an ancient description of what was happening the reader should consult the first six chapters of *Ezra* (skipping chapter 2 unless he has a fascination for long lists of names). We must keep in mind, of course, that the inspired author of the account was giving a religious interpretation of events as he wrote; the book is not historical in our sense of the word. Despite this, we can say that the general picture is an accurate one.

We have seen that "Second Isaiah" had predicted the return from the exile in Babylon. Cyrus, the Persian general (550–530 B.C.), would be the instrument of God's will in this regard (see Is 44:28; 45:1–6). On defeating the Babylonian powers and taking control of the empire, Cyrus instituted new policies with regard to subject nations. Instead of the Assyrian and Babylonian practice of destruction and deportation, he believed in a policy of conciliation. Accordingly, in 539 B.C. he issued a decree permitting all Jewish exiles to return to their homeland and rebuild their temple and cities.

The policy was continued and expanded by Cyrus' successors, Cambyses (530–522 B.C.) and Darius I (522–486 B.C.). As a result, many Jewish pioneers, perhaps several thousand, made the long and difficult trek to the west and homeward. Many were leaving their families, established business and a security achieved after some forty arduous years in exile. But they were moved by profound religious convictions that can make us question the depth and strength of our own. What they found when they reached their destiny hardly justified any joyous celebration. The territory of Judah had been devastated and parts of it appropriated by surrounding peoples; towns and villages were still in disrepair some forty years after the Babylonian conquest; Jerusalem itself and the temple were in ruins; poverty was rampant among those who had been left behind. The sight of all this was hardly encouraging to the weary exiles returned home. It was about the year 536 B.C.

Despite the obstacles, the people, under the leadership of Zerubbabel, a descendant of the royal house of David, and of Jeshua, the priest, gathered at Jerusalem and built first an altar on which proper sacrifice could once more be offered to God. They then laid the foundations for the new temple. On making this propitious beginning, the younger ones especially "shouted with a great shout, praising the Lord, because the foundations of the temple of the Lord were laid." The older ones, however, recalling the magnificence of Solomon's temple, wept at the evident contrast (see Ezra 3). But at least a start had been made in the work of reconstruction.

Still another difficulty was to plague the builders. The Samaritans to the north had heard of the plans to rebuild the temple of Jerusalem. They offered their help in the work, but were sharply rebuffed. Political or religious motives, or both, could have been behind both the offer and its refusal; we cannot be altogether certain. We do know, however, that the Samaritans, smarting under the rebuff, used all means possible to hinder progress; they succeeded admirably (see Ezra 4). For various reasons, including the plots of the Samaritans, work on the temple ceased. This was the situation when "the word of the Lord came through the prophet Haggai."

Some sixteen years had elapsed since the foundations had been laid. By this time the people had salved their consciences sufficiently not to be bothered by the uncompleted house of the Lord. Not so Haggai. "Is it time for you to dwell in your own paneled houses, while this house lies in ruins?" he cried angrily (1:4). And with the backing of Zerubbabel and Jeshua, this man of God succeeded in getting them to work again (1:1–15).

Thus says the Lord of hosts: Consider your ways! Go up into the hill country, bring timber, and build the house that I may take pleasure in it and receive my glory, says the Lord.

You expected much, but it came to little; and what you brought home, I blew away. For what cause? says the Lord of Hosts. Because my house lies in ruins, while each of you hurries to his own house (1:7–9).

The second chapter of this book contains evidence that further prodding was necessary. A month later the prophet rose up and, in the presence of all, admitted that the new temple showed little signs of comparing favorably with Solomon's. They should consider, however, the omnipotent Lord who was with them; His presence is sufficient assurance for the temple's future glory, which will exceed that of the former temple:

For thus says the Lord of hosts: One moment yet, a little while, and I will shake the heavens and the earth, the sea and the dry land.
I will shake all the nations, and the treasures of all the nations will come in, and I will fill this house with glory says the Lord of hosts.
Mine is the silver and mine the gold, says the Lord of hosts.
Greater will be the future glory of this house than the former, says the Lord of hosts; and in this place I will give peace, says the Lord of hosts! (2:6–9).

Two months later still, Haggai spoke more sternly than before in an oracle that seems to condemn the people and the nation for their failure to get on with the work (2:10–14). The final message is one to Zerubbabel, the Jewish leader, encouraging him in his difficult role by painting a glowing picture of his future place in God's plans (2:20–23). The brief oracle has a messianic import that shows that hope had not died out completely in exile.

Haggai must be evaluated in company with his contemporary, Zechariah, to whom the word of the Lord came in the same year. Although Zechariah is not the easiest of the prophets to understand, there are some powerful ideas and powerful expressions in his book. Before saying something about these, we must first note that only chapters 1 to 8 are from the original prophet. As in the book of Isaiah, so here we have a "Second Zechariah," an anonymous prophet (or prophets) to whom the last six chapters are attributed. The core of the original book consists of eight visions (1:7 to 6:15) which are intended both to warn the people of the continuing need for moral reform, and to encourage them in the task of rebuilding temple and city. In his word of warning, Zechariah reads much like the prophets of old whom we have

171

already seen. In fact, the prophet himself says: "Be not like your fathers whom the former prophets warned: Thus says the Lord of hosts: Turn from your evil ways and from your wicked deeds" (1:4).

As you read the descriptions of the visions, try to identify those figures which the prophet uses to symbolize the guilt of Israel or the punishment that hovers over them. The horns, for example, in chapter 2, represent the nations that devastated Judah in the past and were the instruments of her punishment. And the "filthy garments" worn by Jeshua, the priest, are symbolic of Israel's guilt (ch. 3). This persistent awareness of sin and guilt that runs through the prophet's brilliant passages reminds us, too, that, although we live in the Christian era of salvation history, the consciousness of our guilt will heighten our consciousness of God's redeeming grace, of His freely bestowed love.

But Zechariah was no Amos. The concept of punishment is not presented in a way to give a doleful tone to the visions. Throughout we find the encouraging words of the Lord's firm decision to "turn to Jerusalem in mercy" (1:16), "to cast down the horns of the nations that raised their horns to scatter the land of Juda" (2:4), to "take away the guilt of the land in one day" (3:9). Judah and Jerusalem are now in the age of God's mercy and of God's favor. The prophet's insistence on justice and uprightness simply reveal that the ethical demands of old have not been abrogated in the new age.

There are some extremely moving passages in this part of the book. Read aloud the majestic lines of 2:14-17 and try to hear the word with the ears of the returned exiles, discouraged in the task of rebuilding the temple:

Sing and rejoice, O daughter Sion! See, I am coming to dwell among you, says the Lord. Many nations shall join themselves to the Lord on that day, and they shall be his people, and he will dwell among you, and you shall know that the Lord of hosts has sent me to you. The Lord will possess Juda as his portion in the holy land, and he will again choose Jerusalem. Silence, all mankind, in the presence of the Lord! for he stirs forth from his holy dwelling.

Or listen to the joyful words of 8:4–8 and understand what it means to be under the protection of a God such as this:

Thus says the Lord of hosts: Old men and old women, each with staff in hand because of old age, shall again sit in the streets of Jerusalem. The city shall be filled with boys and girls playing in her streets. Thus says the Lord of hosts: Even if this should seem impossible in the eyes of the remnant of this people, shall it in those days be impossible in my eyes also, says the Lord of hosts? Thus says the Lord of hosts: Lo, I will rescue my people from the land of the rising sun, and from the land of the setting sun. I will bring them back to dwell within Jerusalem. They shall be my people, and I will be their God, with faithfulness and justice.

Both Haggai and Zechariah were prophets of a new beginning. Both were concerned with the rebuilding of the temple. And both foresaw a new age in which God would intervene in no uncertain fashion to bring history to its appointed climax. Haggai described this intervention as a shaking of the heavens and the earth, the sea and the dry land, and a shaking of the nations, that would end with the Lord God filling the temple with His glory (2:6–7). Zechariah saw it as the royal coming of the Lord to take possession of His land. So overwhelming will be that act of possession that the solemn charge is given: "Silence, all mankind, in the presence of the Lord! for he stirs forth from his holy dwelling" (Zech 2:17).

It was within this framework that both prophets also saw the royal messiah who had played an important part in the earlier prophets. In the last oracle of Haggai we find another reference to the shaking of the heavens and the earth (2:21), this time accompanied by the designation of Zerubbabel as the Lord's chosen one. Possibly the scion of David's house is seen as a type of the royal messiah to come in the end of days. In Zechariah, too, Zerubbabel looms large in the vision of the future (see 6:9–13):

Thus says the Lord of hosts: Here is a man whose name is Shoot, and where he is he shall sprout, and he shall build the temple of the Lord. Yes, he shall build the temple of the Lord, and taking up the royal insignia, he shall sit as ruler upon his throne. The priest shall be at his right hand, and between the two of them there shall be friendly understanding (6:12–13).

A word must be said here about the last six chapters of *Zechariah,* even though we cannot possibly do them justice in a short space. Most scholars agree that a number of distinct prophecies are contained here, uttered at different times by different men, but almost all of them dating from the period following Alexander the Great's conquest of the Persian world in the latter part of the fourth century B.C. A couple of the oracles are probably the last prophetic utterances of the Old Testament period to be accepted into the canon of Scripture (see 13:1-6). Assured of this late dating, we can then identify the reference to Assyria as a deliberate archaism by which the author concealed from foreign readers the true identity of the object of his remarks. This would be the kingdom of the Seleucids which took over that part of the Alexandrian empire that coincided in part with ancient Assyria. By the same token, the reference to Egypt would be understood by the Jewish readers as a reference to the Ptolemies who now ruled there.

This kind of esoteric writing is a characteristic of the apocalyptic genre which was spawned in time of trouble or persecution and that offered hope to its readers by assurances of victory brought about by divine intervention. The messianic salvation takes on cosmic dimensions and the world powers will war in vain against the new community. One of the most striking of the messianic notes is that the Messiah is here identified, not with all the brilliance and external trappings of the royal court, but with the devout poor who came to be extolled in post-exilic Judaism:

Rejoice heartily, O daughter of Sion, shout for joy, O daughter of Jerusalem! See, your king shall come to you; a just savior is he, meek, and riding on an ass, on a colt, the foal of an ass (9:9).

While the royal nature of the Messiah is not denied, a different picture of it is given than that of the pre-exilic prophets. It is interesting that it is this picture of the royal Messiah that Jesus preferred above all the others (Matt 21:1–9).

Other oracles are difficult to interpret because of the imprecise historical allusions. But the nature of these passages, depicting an assault upon Jerusalem or upon God's people and the ultimate victory to be achieved by God, provided material that would be given a new interpretation in the messianic dispensation to come. Christian readers would immediately recognize those parts of the oracles that were taken up by the New Testament writers. Thus, the ancient author seemingly describes the national mourning for one of those who died heroically in the fighting. The Christian application will be evident:

I will pour out on the house of David and on the inhabitants of Jerusalem a spirit of grace and petition; and they shall look on him whom they have thrust through, and they shall mourn for him as one mourns for an only son, and they shall grieve over him as one grieves over a first-born (12:10).

Two other passages taken over and given new meaning by the New Testament writers will be found in 11:12–13 and 13:7. While many of these later applications may be little more than inspired accommodations of the ancient texts, they attest to a deep conviction concerning the unity and consequent continuity of salvation history. The prophets of old may not have realized how their oracles would be used in the messianic period, but they shared fully this conviction about saving history.

OBADIAH, DENOUNCER OF EDOM

Obadiah (the name means "Servant of Yahweh") is unknown save for his prophecy. This is not too surprising. If a masterful poet like the author of the second part of *Isaiah* could become anonymous within a short time, we should hardly expect to have a complete dossier on the author of the shortest book of the Old Testament. If we give him a date in the fifth century B.C., it is only because he vehemently denounces Edom and Edomites who, during this period, were settling in the southern part of Judah and causing difficulties for the returning exiles. Obadiah shared the prophetic zeal for involvement in the issues of his day, a zeal which can provide a clue for the dating. But even this is far from certain. If the book, short as it is, is divided into distinct passages composed by different writers, as some scholars insist, our problem is multiplied.

But it is a problem we can safely ignore for our purpose. It is sufficient to know something of Edom against whom the attack is leveled. It was an ancient people, as ancient as Israel herself and, according to early Hebrew folklore, was even related to

Israel (see Gen 25 and 36, where the Edomites are presented as descendants of Esau, Jacob's brother). Despite this heralded kinship, the actual relations between the two throughout their history were far from brotherly. From the time when Edom refused Israel permission to cross through her territory (which was to the south and partially east of the Dead Sea) on the way to Canaan (Num 20:14–21), to the post-exilic period when Edom was nagging at Judah's southern border, there was no known period of peaceful and friendly relations. Ever since David's conquest of the land there was a changing pattern of Judaean control (a control that was important if Judah was to have unhindered access to the Gulf of Aqabah and to the Red Sea) and Edomite rebellious independence.

Against this background, any prophet could have found sufficient material for an oracle against the enemy of God's people. Whatever might have been the precise occasion of our present prophecy, Obadiah describes Edom's behavior with regard to Judah in bitter words:

On the day when you stood by, on the day when aliens carried off his possessions, and strangers entered his gates and cast lots over Jerusalem, you too were one of them. Gaze not upon the day of your brother, the day of his disaster; exult not over the children of Juda on the day of their ruin; speak not haughtily on the day of distress! Enter not the gate of my people on the day of their calamity; gaze not, you at least, upon his misfortune on the day of his calamity; lay not hands upon his possessions on the day of his calamity! Stand not at the crossroads to slay his refugees; betray not his fugitives on the day of distress! (vv. 11–14).

The passage could more readily fit the situation shortly after the fall of Jerusalem in 587 B.C. and the subsequent depravation of the land.

But Edom's day would come, the day when the Lord would have His vengeance on this people:

For near is the day of the Lord for all the nations! As you have done, so shall it be done to you, your deed shall come back upon your own head; as you have drunk upon my holy mountain, so shall all the nations drink continually. Yes, they shall drink and swallow, and shall become as though they had not been (vv. 15–16).

The language here is striking, moving with the intensity of Hebrew poetry that loves to lay one image alongside another until the picture is brought indelibly home. Edom shall, like the nations, drink the cup of the Lord's wrath and die.

No such fate for God's people!

But on Mount Sion there shall be a portion saved; the mountain shall be holy, and the house of Jacob shall take possession of those that dispossessed them (v. 17).

It would be unthinkable, of course, that any other future could be in store, not because of the inner worth of God's people, but because of the indomitable and saving power of their God. For better or for worse (and the prophets would have been, and were, the first to admit that the latter was usually the case) He had allied Himself wih Israel. The issue of the alliance could never be total failure.

It is this religious conviction that saves any of the oracles against the nations from being baldly catalogued as narrow, nationalistic invectives without any redeeming qualities. Because he stands squarely, if briefly, in the prophetic tradition, we could legitimately presume this conviction in Obadiah even had he left no verbal evidence of it. But he has left the evidence and it comes, fittingly enough, as the last verse of the prophecy, giving added meaning to all that had gone before:

And saviors shall ascend Mount Sion to rule the mount of Esau,
and the kingship shall be the Lord's (v. 21).

JOEL, PROPHET OF THE SPIRIT

As in the cases of Haggai and Zechariah, so in the case of Joel,
we know little more than his name and the message he brought
to his people. And yet the scholars, with a fair degree of confidence, date the prophecy around the beginning of the fourth
century B.C. The reasons for this date will give us an insight into
the way scholars work and also provide valuable hints for the
interpretation of the book.

One of the first things that strikes the reader of *Joel* is the
strongly apocalyptic tone of the book. By that is meant the use
of highly dramatic imagery to describe cataclysmic events that are
to take place. Chapter 2, for example, is filled with this kind of
writing. The "day of the Lord" (a concept we have already seen
in other prophets) is pictured as "a day of darkness and of
gloom, a day of clouds and somberness" (2:2); there is reference
to the "rumble of chariots," "the crackling of a fiery flame" (2:5),
before which "peoples are in torment" (2:6); "the earth trembles,
the heavens shake; the sun and the moon are darkened, and the
stars withhold their brightness" as "the Lord raises his voice at
the head of his army" (2:10-11).

This is figurative language, of course, designed to arouse a
sense of the Lord's concern and of His impending intervention.
It is a type of writing that was developed rather late in Old
Testament history. The book of *Daniel* is the best example of
apocalyptic literature in the Old Testament, and it was written in
the second century B.C. We do find some traces of apocalyptic

179

writing in the earlier prophets, as for example, in *Isaiah* 24–27, but these are only the stirrings of a literary form that would blossom fully in a much later period. Because *Joel* seems to develop the form more than the earlier prophets, but not as much as *Daniel,* its composition is placed somewhere between the two.

Can we be more specific? In 4:2 the prophet speaks of God's people as being "scattered among the nations." We can be sure, therefore, that the book was composed after the exile had taken place. Still more precisely, in 4:4–6 the prophet accuses the Phoenicians (Tyre and Sidon) and the Philistines of having sold God's people to the Greeks. But the Greeks had no considerable contact with Palestine before the fourth century B.C. The book could not have been composed before that time. It isn't possible to be more exact. It is true that the prophet refers to a great plague of locusts; the plague, in fact, becomes the point of departure for the prophet's message. If we had a record of an especially severe plague of this kind outside the Bible, it might help us to pinpoint the date of Joel. But there is no such record. Besides, there were doubtless many such plagues, as there still are today in that area. Our prophet used one of them as the vehicle of his message.

The first chapter of the book describes in part the devastation wrought by the plague. It is a description that fairly crackles as the prophet pictures the flying insects stripping the stalks of their grain: "for a people has invaded my land, mighty and without number; his teeth are the teeth of a lion, and his molars those of a lioness. He has laid waste my vine, and blighted my fig tree; he has stripped it, sheared off its bark; its branches are made white" (1:6–7). In true prophetic tradition Joel sees this plague as a manifestation of God's anger over the sins of His

180

people. Even in the description of the plague (1:1–12) the words are addressed especially to the "drunkards" and "drinkers of wine" (1:5). In the second part he urges the priests and ministers to "spend the night in sackcloth" (a symbol of mourning) and to "proclaim a fast" (1:13–14). The elders of the people are to be gathered in order to cry to the Lord for mercy.

It is at this point that the prophet begins to see much more than a natural plague. It becomes now the prefiguring of that terrible day to come, the day of the Lord (see 1:15). But he continues, for a few verses (1:16–20), to describe the locust plague before veering off into a description of *the* day (2:1–11). It is a powerful passage, deserving of being read aloud in order that the words of impending doom might receive their fullest accent. It is a mighty picture of the transcendent Lord and of His all-consuming power:

Blow the trumpet in Sion, sound the alarm on my holy mountain! Let all who dwell in the land tremble, for the day of the Lord is coming; yes, it is near, a day of darkness and of gloom a day of clouds and somberness!

Like dawn spreading over the mountains, a people numerous and mighty!

Their like has not been from of old, nor will it be after them, even to the years of distant generations. Before them a fire devours, and after them a flame enkindles; like the garden of Eden is the land before them and after them a desert waste; from them there is no escape.

Their appearance is that of horses; like steeds they run.

As with the rumble of chariots they leap on the mountaintops; as with the crackling of a fiery flame devouring stubble; like a mighty people arrayed for battle.

Before them peoples are in torment, every face blanches. Like warriors they run, like soldiers they scale the wall; they advance, each in his own lane, without swerving from their paths.

181

No one crowds another, each advances in his own track; though they fall into the ditches, they are not checked. They assault the city, they run upon the wall, they climb into the houses; in at the windows they come like thieves.

Before them the earth trembles, the heavens shake; the sun and the moon are darkened, and the stars withhold their brightness.

The Lord raises his voice at the head of his army; for immense indeed is his camp, yes, mighty, and it does his bidding.

For great is the day of the Lord, and exceedingly terrible; who can bear it? (2:1-11).

But Joel does not remain in this apocalyptic framework. Like all prophets he is a man involved, and he must make his application to his own people. He calls on them to repent, to "proclaim a fast, call an assembly . . . and say, 'Spare, O Lord, your people . . .' " (2:15–17) Even the day of the Lord to come can be an inducement to the people of the present to return to their Lord. In much the same way St. Paul used the picture of the second and glorious coming of Jesus Christ to stir up the Christians of his day. Joel's description of the God of penitent people contrasts vividly with that of the God of sinners:

Yet even now, says the Lord, return to me with your whole heart, with fasting, and weeping, and mourning; rend your hearts, not your garments, and return to the Lord, your God.

For gracious and merciful is he, slow to anger, rich in kindness, and relenting in punishment (2:12–13).

The prophet then describes the fruit of true conversion. It is the stirring of the Lord to concern for His land and to pity for His people (2:18). Using the same basic imagery as before, he reveals how God will now shower His blessings on the land:

Fear not, O land! exult and rejoice! for the Lord has done great things.

Fear not, beasts of the field! for the pastures of the plain are green; the tree bears its fruit, the fig tree and the vine give their yield. The threshing floors shall be full of grain and the vats shall overflow with wine and oil (2:21–22, 24).

For the prophets of Israel the imagery of the land, either as barren or as fruitful, was the principal figure of divine punishment or reward. This is natural enough because it is an imagery the people could readily understand. The fruitfulness of the land was an absolute necessity for physical existence; it was an appropriate figure of spiritual well being.

Continuing in the same vein, Joel now specifies the messianic blessings as the outpouring of the spirit of God:

Then afterward I will pour out my spirit upon all mankind. Your sons and daughters shall prophesy, your old men shall dream dreams, your young men shall see visions; even upon the servants and the handmaids, in those days, I will pour out my spirit (3:1–2).

On Pentecost Sunday, St. Peter, in addressing the Jewish people who had crowded into Jerusalem for the feast day, proclaimed the prophecy of Joel fulfilled. The Spirit of God had come down upon the twelve and transformed them from a terrified group of men, cowering behind locked doors "for fear of the Jews," into courageous witnesses to the resurrection of Jesus of Nazareth. The messianic time of fulfillment had arrived (see Acts 2:14–17).

The spirit of God is an important concept in the theology of the Bible. It is a concept that underwent a long development. In the oldest parts of the Old Testament it is seen as a special power that comes from God and that enables men to do extraordinary things. For example, the spirit of God came down upon Samson and gave him the strength to tear a "lion in pieces as one tears a kid" (Judges 14:6). In the same way did it seize hold of Gideon and Jephthah and Saul. In those men, however, who play a dominant role in Old Testament history throughout their lives, the spirit of God does not come down in sporadic instances. Rather, it rests upon them in such a way that it becomes characteristic of them. The spirit of God was permanently in Moses and could be described as being shared also by those who were to help him in his work (see Num 11:17). Again, when Samuel anointed the young David in pledge of his future kingship, we read that "the spirit of the Lord came upon David from that day forward" (1 Sam 16:13).

The spirit of God, therefore, was nothing else but the manifestation of God's grace working in these favored persons of the Old Testament. It is only natural, then, that the future messianic prince should also be described as sharing in the spirit of God, even to a special degree. Isaiah describes him in these words: "The spirit of the Lord shall rest upon him: a spirit of wisdom and of understanding, a spirit of counsel and of strength, a spirit of knowledge and of fear of the Lord . . ." (11:2). Even in exile, our anonymous "Second Isaiah" kept alive the theology of the spirit of God by describing the servant of Yahweh as one with whom the Lord is pleased, "upon whom I have put my spirit; he shall bring forth justice to the nations . . ." (42:1). The presence of God's spirit is the necessary condition for the preaching of the good news of salvation (Is 61:1).

In none of these passages, it must be insisted, was the spirit of God seen as a distinct person. If some of the descriptions seem to indicate a person, this is only because the Hebrew people preferred concrete and vivid pictures to abstract concepts. Personification was one means of being concrete and vivid. It was only in the New Testament period, after the revelation of the Son of God, that there was a gradual understanding of the Spirit of God as a distinct person. The revelation was to play a large part in St. Paul's theology. Joel had prepared for this later development by his identification of the outpouring of the spirit of God with the messianic age. He had taken a notion already handled in other prophecies, and gave it the fullest extension possible in the confines of the Old Testament.

MALACHI AND THE PERFECT SACRIFICE

. . . for from the rising of the sun, even to its setting, my name is great among the nations; and everywhere they bring sacrifice to my name, and a pure offering; for great is my name among the nations, says the Lord of hosts (Mal 1:11).

This passage from the prophet Malachi is familiar to all who have studied their Catholic catechisms. It is presented, usually, as a clear prediction of the sacrifice of the Mass and hence as proof that the Mass was foreseen by Israel's prophets and willed by God. Unfortunately the presentation frequently neglects entirely the context in which the passage is found and the historical background of its formulation. When we study that context and that background we shall see how amazing the statement really is.

First, let us see something of our prophet and his book. Actually we know very little of the man himself, not even his name! "Malachi" is a Hebrew word meaning "my messenger" and indicates that the prophet is one chosen by God to deliver the divine message. Some have suggested that he did not want to reveal his true identity out of fear of those about whom he had some very harsh things to say. Or the later editor may have given the book this name because of the statement in 3:1: "Lo, I am sending *my messenger* to prepare the way before me; and suddenly there will come to the temple the Lord whom you seek, and the messenger of the covenant whom you desire. Yes, he is coming, says the Lord of hosts."

The oracles were delivered in the post-exilic period. We know that from 1:8 where he uses the word "governor," a term used by the Persians who did govern the land in the period after the exile. The fact that the priests were offering sacrifices and conducting temple services shows that the temple had been restored, and it was finished in 515 B.C. The increased abuses in worship suggest that some years had passed since the enthusiastic renewal of the temple liturgy. And the prevalence of divorce and mixed marriages shows that the reforms of Ezra and Nehemiah had not yet been instituted. From all this it is concluded that the prophecies were delivered shortly before the middle of the fifth century B.C., *about* 460.

There seems to have been some grumbling among the people about the economic situation. They are pictured as complaining that they carry out their religious practices, offering sacrifices and paying tithes, but God doesn't seem to answer (see 1:6–7). Since God says that, when these practices are carried out *properly,* He will answer by forbidding the locust to destroy their crops and the vine to be barren (3:11), we can suppose that these conditions were the actual reasons for their complaint.

How does Malachi answer them? First of all, he assures them that God has not ceased loving them. That love is starkly stated by way of contrast, a favorite biblical device to emphasize a point. Here it is made by saying that "I loved Jacob (who represents all the Jewish people), but hated Esau (who represents all the Edomites, Israel's enemies living to the south)" (1:3). At the time, Edom was apparently undergoing invasion by the

186

Nabataeans who gradually established themselves in the land (see 1:4–5). According to the prophet, the relative security of the Jews was an indication of God's love.

On the other hand, if they are suffering material want, he assures them that there are excellent reasons for the absence of God's blessings. One of these is the slipshod manner in which the priests are practicing the liturgy. They have grown so callous in their sacred office that they actually offer victims to God that are lame or sick or unfit in some way. The law was very strict on this point (see Lev 22:17–25). Their strictness flowed from Israel's high regard for the holiness of God who was being worshipped. It is in this context that Malachi's statement, given at the beginning, was made. He says that, in contrast to the unworthy offerings made by Israel's priests, those of the pagan nations are pure and acceptable. This is surely a tremendous statement coming from the mouth of a Jewish writer, from one who was convinced that God, in comparison with His great love for Israel, hated the pagan nation of Edom. It shows, first of all, that that hatred is not taken literally, but also that pagan worship could be conceived as an unconscious worship of the one God, Yahweh. What, then, of the Church's teaching that there is a reference here to the sacrifice of the Mass? Malachi himself could not have foreseen that sacrifice. But he could have foreseen that the pure worship of the Gentiles of his day was a foreshadowing of a perfect sacrifice that would one day truly be offered "from the rising of the sun, even to its setting," that is, everywhere in the world. The Council of Trent, which quoted these words in its discussion of the Mass, has applied them to a new reality which is in the same order of revelation and which therefore can be said to find meaningful roots in the ancient realities.

In some ancient translations the words are placed in the future, and in this case Malachi would be consciously looking forward to a pure and acceptable sacrifice not yet realized in the Jewish sacrifice. But the original Hebrew wording is better translated in the present tense, as we read it in our modern Bibles. Even so, that a Jewish prophet could make this statement at a time when the nationalistic spirit was very strong is remarkable enough. It is one more bit of evidence for the remarkable character of the prophetic movement in the Old Testament. The prophets could always be counted on to strike hard at complacency and triumphalism. In this sense the Fathers of the Second Vatican Council shared the spirit of Israel's prophets.

Malachi was not content to condemn the sacrificial victims; he condemned also the priests who offered them (2:1-9). In some rather strong language (typical of the prophets) he describes what their fate will be unless they reform:

And now, O priests, this commandment is for you: If you do not listen, and if you do not lay it to heart, to give glory to my name, says the Lord of hosts, I will send a curse upon you and of your blessing I will make a curse. Yes, I have already cursed it, because you do not lay it to heart (2:1-2).

He goes on to picture the ideal priest and what can be expected of such a one. The Catholic priest of today still looks back to these words of Malachi to measure his own way with the Lord:

My covenant with him was one of life and peace; fear I put in him, and he feared me, and stood in awe of my name.

True doctrine was in his mouth, and no dishonesty was found upon his lips; he walked with me in integrity and uprightness, and turned many away from evil.

For the lips of the priest are to keep knowledge, and instruction

188

is to be sought from his mouth, because he is the messenger of the Lord of hosts (2:5-7).

The laity, too, come in for their share of prophetic denunciation. We have already mentioned the evils of divorce and mixed marriages that were prevalent at the time. Malchi's reference to them is a masterpiece of deep religious concern and of high regard for the natural beauty of marriage. The situation seemed to be that Jewish men were divorcing their Jewish wives and marrying pagan women (see Ezra 9:1–2.12; 10:1–3, where the reform is introduced). The reform instituted by Ezra and Nehemiah was being prepared by the oracles of Malachi. He first refers to the unity of the people under God the Father: "Have we not all the one Father? Has not the one God created us? Why then do we break faith with each other, violating the covenant of our fathers?" (2:10). This unity, sealed by the covenant of Sinai, bespeaks a strong bond also between Israelite and Israelite. This bond has been weakened, if not broken, by marriage to "an idolatrous woman," or, as the Hebrew text reads literally, "the daughter of a strange god."

The prophet has given the highest religious motivation to his condemnation. The holiness of Yahweh is profaned by the presence of pagan elements among His people: "Juda has broken faith; an abominable thing has been done in Israel and in Jerusalem. Juda has profaned the temple which the Lord loves, and has married an idolatrous woman" (2:11). Moreover, God looks forward, in the true Israelite marriage, to a "godly offspring" (2:15). But is this not jeopardized by marriage to pagans?

Equally moving is his appeal to avoid divorce. He here provides a strong Scriptural basis for the unity of marriage. In reply to their question why God does not accept their sacrifices he answers: ". . . because the Lord is witness between you and the wife of your youth, with whom you have broken faith though she is your companion, your betrothed wife" (2:13–14). He appeals here both to their religious sensibilities inasmuch as the Lord Himself is said to be a witness to the marriage, and to their sense of justice inasmuch as they married their Jewish wives when the latter were young and fair, and now wish to repudiate their contract. It seems, then, that Malachi does not look kindly even on the provision for divorce in some particular cases given by the Law (see Deut 24:1–5). "For I hate divorce, says the Lord, the God of Israel . . ." (2:16). Such a strong condemnation can be seen as an inspired commentary on *Genesis* 2:24 and an ideal preparation for the equally strong statement of Jesus in *Mark* 10:2–9.

The last verse of chapter 2 explains why the Lord is wearied with His people. They have become cynical, questioning the justice of God. The attitude is the occasion for the prophet's description of the day of the Lord. Like Amos, Malachi says that the day will be a dreadful one for many: "But who will endure the day of his coming? And who can stand when he appears? For he is like the refiner's fire, or like the fuller's lye" (3:2). But unlike Amos, he does not dwell almost exclusively on the doom that will overtake the sinners. Rather, he depicts as well the blessings that will come to the faithful and to those who turn to the Lord on that day. Do what is right and then "try me," says the Lord, "shall I not open for you the floodgates of heaven, to pour down blessings upon you without measure?" (3:10).

In his final words, Malachi says that God will send Elijah, the prophet, "before the day of the Lord comes . . . to turn the hearts of the fathers to their children, and the hearts of the children to their fathers . . ." (3:23). This is the messenger mentioned in the first verse of this same chapter, quoted above; Jesus saw the description fulfilled in John the Baptist (Matt 11:10). These are the last words in the collection of great prophetical books. It seems appropriate that they should be words of expectation, of looking forward to the time of fulfillment. It is appropriate, too, that Elijah, one of the great prophets of the Old Testament, should figure in this final note of hope.